Surviving the Axe

First published in 2009 by
Liberties Press
Guinness Enterprise Centre | Taylor's Lane | Dublin 8
Tel: +353 (1) 415 1224
www.LibertiesPress.com | info@libertiespress.com

Distributed in the United States by
Dufour Editions | PO Box 7 | Chester Springs | Pennsylvania | 19425

and in Australia by
James Bennett Pty Limited | InBooks | 3 Narabang Way
Belrose NSW 2085

Trade enquiries to CMD Distribution
55A Spruce Avenue | Stillorgan Industrial Park
Blackrock | County Dublin
Tel: +353 (1) 294 2560 | Fax: +353 (1) 294 2564

ISBN: 978–1–905483–60–0
2 4 6 8 10 9 7 5 3 1

A CIP record for this title is available from the British Library.

Cover design by Ros Murphy
Internal design by Liberties Press
Printed in Ireland by Colour Books | Baldoyle Industrial Estate | Dublin 13

Surviving the Axe

The Irish Guide to Handling Redundancy and Finding a New Job

Lisa O'Callaghan

LIB
ERT
IES

To Cormac and Ryan

Contents

IT'S A RECESSION WHEN YOUR NEIGHBOUR LOSES HIS JOB;
IT'S A DEPRESSION WHEN YOU LOSE YOUR OWN.

HARRY S. TRUMAN

1

How Did We Get Here?

While cruising around the magnificent Ha Long bay in Vietnam on my honeymoon, something was revealed about the state of my inner world. Something curious. Living in such close quarters with other passengers eventually led to the inevitable question: 'What do you do?' A simple enough question, we all agree. And you would also think, being away from home and real life, and among travellers from all corners of the globe with no more on their mind than what local delicacies their next meal may consist of, you would think that the answer – 'I'm not working right now' – would be pretty painless. But to my surprise, it wasn't: the answer got stuck in my throat.

You could also assume that, with my broad experience as a 'serial unemployee', I would be well used to the question and remain ever ready with a repertoire of light-hearted and witty returns: 'I'm not working right now, I'm on a witness protection programme'; 'I'm not working, my job died and I'm observing a period of mourning'; 'I'm not working; I'm recovering from a tough mission to Mars' or 'a debilitating mental disorder' – or, for my less adventurous days – 'training for the Olympics'. And so forth.

But no. Each time I was asked 'So . . . what do you do?', a little piece of me died as I choked out the words

'I'm not working right now', with a smile that said: 'Please kill me now and put me out of my misery'.

So what is this anxiety all about? There was a time in Ireland – and not so long ago, either – when if you said you had a job, everyone would stare at you in wonder. People would point you out to their friends in the corridor. As for the rest of us highly-trained graduates, the dole queue off Parnell Street was *the* place to hang out. As a country, we were very intimately attached to our reputation as having the highest unemployment rate in Europe . . . ever. There was no shame, no embarrassment, attached to this state of affairs, just calm acceptance of our status as the unemployment hub of the European Union.

But then everything went wrong. We crawled out of a hundred-year depression and got rich! Got prosperous. Got jobs – good jobs – and exciting careers in fast-growth industries like biotechnology and telecoms, software and pharmaceuticals. And off we all went, with our proverbial oxtail soup and egg sandwiches, and strapped ourselves in on the roller coaster that is – or rather, *was* – the infamous Celtic Tiger.

And of course, with our new-found prosperity, bad things happened. We went and got spoilt, didn't we – presumptuous, even. We started asking for pay rises and didn't have to pretend we had a better offer – we did . . . lots of them. Share options replaced the price of a pint as the main topic of conversation. Our careers went from being non-existent to the reason for our existence.

Fast-forward a few short years and, as it is with all historical tragedies, we have come full circle. Remember the downturn of 2002? No? Well, you must have been working! I do, unfortunately. Recession only happens to those who lose their jobs! That was the global telecoms meltdown which sent tens of thousands of talented individuals here in Ireland back to the place they thought they would never see again in their lifetime. No, not the 1990 Euro Cup finals – the dole queue! Or for the luckier ones, the airport check-in desk, to look for work abroad.

And here we are again, facing a downturn to beat all downturns, which threatens not only our jobs but also pretty much everything else we have all worked so hard to create. (And I'm not just talking about your collection of designer shoes, I'm also talking about your livelihood, your pensions and investments, your net worth!) That's if you choose to believe the statistics. In addition to the dismal economic forecasts, unemployment forecasts are heading for 11 percent in 2010. On first view, you might think 'Well, it's only 11 percent' – until you realise that this is triple what it was in 2005, and equates to approximately 350,000 talented and bright individuals with no jobs to go to. If that isn't enough to give you the heebie-jeebies, no-one is putting bets on any real improvement taking place until well into 2011.

If you haven't by now reached for the Valium, you're probably clear-headed enough to ask yourself that all-important question: what should I do about it? What can I do if, one day, I hear those dreaded words: 'I have some bad news about your role.'

To be made redundant is, to quote every theory on stress-related illness, one of the most traumatic things ever to befall you. It's right up there with death of a loved one, divorce and terminal illness!

It was during the previously mentioned 2002 telecoms meltdown, when I and almost all of my work colleagues at that time assumed the job title of 'professional reject' or 'redundee'. And as an experienced redundee, I have had occasions to mull over this so-called devastating event with a mix of amusement, insight, angst and denial (a most under-rated life skill).

Herein lie the observations made, survival tips learned and borrowed from my many redundant comrades, truths I should have known but didn't and mistakes I made as I made my way through the valley of the disappearing ego. I survived to tell the tale, with no discernible social disorder. Or perhaps I am currently in 'remission' and will be led to the door at any moment.

If you are currently seeking employment, in reading this I am sure you will get comfort from the experiences of the many who have gone before you . . . and survived. Remember that you too will come back stronger.

If you've never lost your job and are reading this purely to entertain yourself: welcome aboard, you never know when you too may get 'a visit'. It's good to be prepared.

My Career as an Unemployee

Most of us have experienced unemployment at some point in our lives, from the easy times following graduation, or a return from travelling, to the more difficult times, such as being let go during an economic downturn. And job loss is particularly prevalent among those of us who started working early. From running errands for a tuppence piece, delivering papers, picking strawberries, serving chips or pulling pints, we've all done our fair share of back-breaking labour for less than the minimum wage. And when one of these jobs ends, it tends not to be life-changing: mildly irritating, perhaps, but not traumatic.

It is later in life when losing your job hurts: for some people, the experience is so upsetting that they never quite recover from it. But whenever it happened, either early or late, every redundee I have spoken to learned valuable lessons from their journey in and out of unemployment. And this is also true for me.

Before I had secured my first 'real' job in my mid-twenties, I'd experienced job loss several times. This may sound bad, but it must be said that the first incident occurred when I was six years old. Back then, I was fired from a job I loved and in which I took immense pride – posting letters for Sister Magdelene, my teacher. Sister Magdalene was a gentle and sweet lady and I loved her, as did all the other kids. I can't quite remember how I got the job of posting her pale blue envelopes, but I think the fact the school was over-run with my siblings meant that the odds were always going to be in our favour.

It started wonderfully and, at the risk of sounding boastful, I was excellent at my job. I showed up on time, waited patiently outside her door, tucked her envelopes into a safe pocket of my bag where the fizzy drinks could never touch them, and ran like the hammers of hell to the post office. There, I purchased the required stamps and, with the seriousness of a brain surgeon, slobbered enough saliva on them to cause a flood, before dispatching the sacred blue items into the little green postbox outside. When I returned triumphant, I would be rewarded with a saintly smile and a tuppence piece, which was a lot in those days.

This first stab at independence came to a crashing end one drizzling spring day when I agreed to take my new friend, Ms X, with me. As we walked along the river, heated words were exchanged over something I cannot recall, and I received a shove towards the water. In my effort to stay on dry land, I dropped my bag into the wild water and watched in horror as the envelopes floated out of their safe place and off on their own journey. Despite several (quite dangerous) rescue attempts, my cargo was lost. Needless to say, Sister Magdelene was appalled, particularly at my pathetic efforts at lying about the incident, and before I could shout 'It was all Ms X's fault',

Ms X's cousin was brought in to replace me (that's small towns for you!). Sister Magdelene never spoke to me again and I never spoke to Ms X! I spent the tuppence pay-off on four huge green-and-red gobstoppers.

Lesson learned: Never take any passengers . . . oh, and, I suppose . . . work first, fight later!

Three years and two jobs later, at the grand old age of nine, it happened again. This time it was plain and simple fraudulent practice – sneaking little stones into the strawberry bucket to increase its weight, and hence my earnings. You know, it was just one of those things that you assumed everyone else was doing too because it just seemed so obvious. But like all useless criminals, I eventually got complacent and more generous with the amount of stones I was using. In fact, I piled them in, in front of the farmer. The walk home to my disappointed parents was a tough one!

Lesson learned: Crime doesn't pay as well as it should!

The next time was ten years later, and it could be categorized as your typical student summer experience. I was working in North America on a Student J1 working-holiday visa as one of three Irish girls in a busy restaurant. We were proud of our reputation as hardworking, reliable and, of course, good craic. Unfortunately, the new manager didn't think so when she realised we would not be around for the busiest weekend of the year the following month.

My friend was fired loudly as she walked through the door a few mornings later. I was fired at that point too – in my absence, though. I was still languishing in my cockroach-infested bed, trying to decide between a morning of shopping or one spent lounging on the beach, when she arrived home with the news.

We were so indignant at our loss of our final two weeks' earnings, we did the typical Irish thing and told absolutely everybody about the terrible, *terrible* injustice which had befallen us.

Lesson learned: Present reliability doesn't pay as well as future availability!

The last experience before my proper working career began was at a small research company, over the manager's request for me to make her a cup of coffee. I said 'I'm busy right now', and there was no more work left for me to do. Oops!

Lesson learned: Sometimes it's worth it!

And there ended my early experiences of being made redundant. Subsequently, from my mid-twenties to my mid-thirties, I experienced two bouts of redundancy and, yes, the later experiences were completely different from the early ones. First of all, I cared a lot about my jobs and the companies I worked for – both in the fast-changing technology and services industries, which carry their own risks and rewards. And secondly, I had developed into a professional manager and it was thus more difficult to pick up the pieces and start again. The inspiration for writing this book was derived from these later experiences.

2

You're It!

Handling Job Loss

LOSS IS NOTHING ELSE BUT CHANGE, AND
CHANGE IS NATURE'S DELIGHT
J. M. BARRIE

LOSS IS NOTHING BUT A PAIN IN THE NECK, AND IF IT IS IN-
DEED NATURE'S DELIGHT, SHE HAS A SICK SENSE OF HUMOUR
LISA O'CALLAGHAN

It always sucks when you lose your job, especially when you have no other job to go to. Even when you hated it, thought your boss had stepped out of a scene from *The Office* and believed that the place carried a strange smell of dead animals. Yes, it always hurts, and invariably leaves you with a sense of failure. Sometimes you see it coming and can mentally prepare for it, to help ease the pain. Sometimes you don't suspect a thing and feel like you are caught in one of those candid-camera TV programmes, because everything seems so surreal.

Redundancy and the threat of it is a stranger beast again, because it brings out a wide array of characteristics in people. But one thing is for sure: both you and people around you will change once the threat begins to approach. This is understandable. We tend to work a little harder, for a start! But something else happens too.

And it's not always bad. Sometimes it is downright funny: certain personality types emerge. In my experience, these can be categorised into ten distinct types:

1. THE ESCAPED PRISONER

These are the ones with a sense of wide-eyed urgency and ready smiles (and sometimes raucous laughter), their calculators constantly clicking, totting up how much they plan to earn with their pay-off, and helping others tot up theirs. They're hoping, praying, it'll be them. If a voluntary-redundancy package is on offer, they are first up. The Escaped Prisoners hate their jobs, may have something else lined up, want to travel, or just want to be at home for a while. Nothing, but nothing, is going to come between them and the pay-off. These are often the best people to hang with. They're not interested in playing games, back-stabbing, or any kind of manipulation, except that which will lead them out. The only downside for you is that their enthusiasm about the prospect of leaving may infect you. If you genuinely want to stay, don't let yourself be swept away by it. In this group, you tend to find working mothers with young children, anyone under twenty-six, and finance and accounts personnel.

2. THE PANIC MERCHANT

'It's us, it's us, it's me and you and you. I know it is. I know it is. I saw them looking at us when they came out of their meeting. They turned their eyes away from me when I passed. It's definitely gonna be from this group. Def-in-itely. Mary from Accounts thinks the same thing. So does Paul in IT. We're doomed . . . *doomed!'*

Unfortunately, it's illegal to shoot people, but if you could, these would definitely be the first people against the wall. They will break your heart. They will wreck your head. They will drive not only themselves but also you to paranoid psychosis. Don't have coffee with them – or lunch – and if you do, tell them they can't mention the 'R' word. Panic merchants tend to be either relatively new or just insecure. They may have jobs with no clearly defined responsibilities. They most often don't like or don't trust their boss. But the strange thing about Panic Merchants is . . . they tend to be right!

3. THE FANTASIST

'It'll never be me. I'm too important. My boss loves me too much. They'd be lost without me. I'm the one who keeps this company together. If it hadn't been for me . . .' The Fantasist acts as if nothing is happening, laughs at others' anxiety and carries on with their request for the latest phone, a business trip to Taiwan, a training day in the Four Seasons. They will tell you not to worry and that it's going to be someone else. People in this group tend to be young graduates or old-timers, or on drugs: in other words, too young, too old, or too spaced to know better. Don't be fooled.

4. THE BORN-AGAIN CONSCIENTIOUS

This is where monthly sick days, 9.30 AM-ish starts and long-winded explanations on why nothing ever happens are suddenly replaced with rude health, zealous time-keeping and regular, loud updates on 'achievements'. Annoying? Yes. My advice? swallow your pride and do some PR of your own. And let's face it. We could all work a little harder.

5. THE PROTECTED SPECIES

We know them and hate them: the ones who know that no matter what happens, it ain't gonna happen to them. You recognise them in their false concern and all-too-ready cheery smile; their regular coffee breaks with the head honchos to discuss how much territory will be

20

given over to them when Ms X or Mr Y gets the boot; their insistence that all of the bad things that are happening are good and healthy and that we're all better off without our jobs anyway. The Protected Species has nothing to say about the state of the jobs market or recruitment agencies, because they haven't looked: they haven't needed to. They always insist on changing the subject when the conversation turns to the topic of redundancy, because 'It's sooo boring'. People in this category tend to be the boss's offspring, the boss's protégés, long-time faithful servants, or top salespeople. Advice: get to know them or, better still, find some embarrassing information on them, and their protective coat may save you too.

6. The Escape Artist

It would be worth doing a full anthropological study of the Escape Artist, because we have much to learn from them. Unlike the Protected Species, they have no connection to anyone in particular, no golden reputation with which to blind employers, in fact no real reason to be there in the first place! I have a dear friend who has managed to avoid five redundancy programmes in the space of two years without ever having any specific job specification or, believe it or not, much to do! But each time redundancy seems imminent, the hatchet man just passes him by. Amazing! I bow to these people. They are true survivors, and every company who has them should listen to them, for they are wise and knowing people who will never go hungry. People in this category tend to be quiet (*very* quiet!) but still manage to know, and be known by, everyone.

7. The Friendly Assassin

Have you ever had someone approach you on the quiet to explain that 'sticking together' is the best way to hold on to your job? Have you ever had anyone promise that they will 'watch your back' while they are actively trying to get rid of other people? Well, we've seen enough TV survival shows to know that we should treat such people with great suspicion: you're probably the one they're after. The way to handle someone like that is to appear to go along with them, and confidently say things like: 'We all agree that it's the best way . . . I have to go to a meeting now but, rest assured, I will watch your back too.' Make him wonder: one, where you're going; two, who you're meeting, and three (most important of all), who's 'we'?

8. THE BLEEDING HEART

These people will look for any excuse to get out of being treated as an equal target for the hatchet man. Whether their plea is 'But I've only just arrived', 'But I've only just bought a house' or 'But I've only just found out I'm pregnant', you can be sure that preferential treatment will be meted out to them. Advice: get in there with your own sob story. Even the hatchet man has a heart.

9. THE MORAL MAJORITY

This species will huddle in groups for hours and talk about the poor unfortunates who got the chop as if they had died. Hushed tones, bowed heads, even a tear or two. Perhaps there's a little bit of survivor's guilt and a few grains of genuine concern, but really they're just bloody relieved that it wasn't them. If they truly cared as much as that, they'd act on it in some way. And some do: I'm happy to report that I've met them.

10. THE LEGAL EAGER

Against the threat of redundancy, some people run to their calculators, and others run to the pub, but you can always be sure that some will run to their solicitors.

Sometimes, if handled correctly, that can be a smart move. But Legal Eagers will speak loud and proud about it, and sometimes even parade their solicitor around the place like a prized bull. Legal Eagers are great for the after-work gossip-fest and are welcome at any table. People in this category tend to be those who have massive egos or who have genuinely been badly treated.

The Redundancy Process

Some people have a nice, fair boss who, gently and without prejudice, pulls them aside to explain that the role they occupy will be made redundant in a number of weeks' or months' time, explains the reasons clearly (and you believe them), glows about your performance without needing to be asked, and offers a strong reference and job referrals. There is often a tasty severance package too. These are good honest folk. You can tell they do not want to do what they are doing, and you almost want to put a comforting arm around them to reassure them.

The only reaction to a situation like that is to maintain the strong relationship you have with your boss, in the hope that if an opportunity comes up again, he or she will consider you first. You do this by accepting the situation with dignity and offering supportive words towards your boss and the company – hard though it may be to do so.

While this chapter is useful for all types of redundancy situations, it caters, in particular, for a certain company approach. I like to call it: 'All Prisoners up Against the Wall'. The company is cutting back on staff and letting people know in quick-fire procession that they have lost their job. Managers tend to do this by either calling a big group meeting or summoning people into their office, one after the other and often with little or no warning, to utter the dreaded words: 'I have some bad news about your role.' This practice is ruthlessly efficient, but cold. It is also typical of large organisations and companies that are going down the tubes. For example, in one redundancy situation I experienced, we were told that between 10 AM and 2 PM, 150 people would be let go, and that all personnel should be at their desks during these hours, in case they were to receive a call. Lovely!

More and more these days, I meet people who were made redundant using this 'gunfire' approach. This chapter is dedicated to those who find themselves waiting against the proverbial wall, wondering if the gun is being aimed at them.

1. AWAITING THE CALL

So, hatchet time has arrived and you've all congregated at your desks, hands joined in a hip-hop version of 'Nearer My God to Thee', hoping and praying that it isn't going to be you who gets 'the call' (no, not from God calling you into the religious order – the call from your boss to tell you to clear off). Everyone is on edge, their heart jumping into their mouth at anything that even sounds like a phone ringing. Those who wanted to go have already gone. If you've had some prior warning, your bags are already semi-packed, the confidential company information dispatched to its secret hiding place under your sweater, your coffee mug cleaner than it's ever been . . . and then . . . uh-oh, what's that you hear? Brrrinng Brrrinng . . . Brrrinng Brrrinng . . . It's for you-oooooo! Well . . . you gotta answer it. You don't wanna. But you gotta.

I won't bore you with the polite, professional way of answering the telephone: we've been trained how to do that from birth. However, here's how the call could go if you're feeling brave:

(During redundancy, mild cases of light-hearted rude-ness will be tolerated, so take full advantage.)

YOU:	RMS Titanic, how can I help?
HATCHET MAN:	Ahem . . . oh, hello . . . is that Lisa?'
YOU:	It's Captain Smith, and you must be the iceberg they were warning me about. (*It's OK. You're allowed to be cheeky, you're getting the boot, remember!*)
HATCHET MAN:	Ha Ha. Yes. So, Lisa . . . do you think, Lisa, you could come to see us (*Us! never a good thing to hear!*), whenever you're ready, Lisa?

(I've never actually figured out why, when someone wants to tell you bad news, they use your name *a lot*.) *Long drawn out silence as he awaits your response.*

'Mild' and 'light-hearted' are the important words here. Aggression, violence, or the threat of violence – in fact any form of threatening behaviour, deeply tempting though it is – is a big fat no-no!

2. PUT THE PHONE DOWN FIRST. QUICK. HURRY. SLAM IT

Believe it or not, this little thing helps re-establish your own power. Or try this one: don't slam the phone down. Just put your little finger down to disconnect the line, and keep talking:

'Oh that is fant*aaaa*stic!! . . . *How* much? *Nooo*! When do I start?'

Turn to your colleagues and scream: 'I got it!'

Then throw your puckered lips around the place in a group-air kiss, and skip – don't walk, skip – out of the office.

Or, if neither of those reactions agrees with you, just 'fess up and say: 'F**k it! . . . The f**kers!' and wallow in everyone's fake sympathy for as long as you can stomach it.

3. DON'T HANG AROUND: THE REDUNDANCY VIRUS COULD BE AIRBORNE

Quickly email anyone who might care and tell them that you'll be in touch, then say your goodbyes and leave. You are now the leper no one wants to touch. I mean, can you actually prove that the redundancy virus is not airborne? Now is not a time for anyone to take any chances. Anyway, your colleagues want you to go because they want to gossip about you. So shoo!

TOP TIPS IN HANDLING THE DREADED PHONE CALL REQUEST TO COME TO THE EXECUTION ROOM

Light-hearted cheekiness will be tolerated, so don't be afraid to have a little fun.

Put the phone down first. This helps to re-establish your power. I don't know why, it just does.

Don't hang around. The Redundancy Virus could be airborne.

Don't cry or scream within a one-mile radius.

Keep them waiting (a little).

Take ten long deep breaths before you enter the room. It will keep you calm

4. ONLY CRY OR SCREAM OUTSIDE A ONE-MILE RADIUS OF THE BUILDING

This goes without saying. Don't cry or scream – which makes people laugh or cry, and only adds to the gossip.

5. KEEP THEM WAITING

Don't rush to your execution. Trust me, they're going nowhere. Have a little wander, take your time in the toilet to blow your nose, take a pee, call your partner *and* your best friend in Saudi Arabia (well, that mobile phone will not be yours in about two minutes' time!), let the agencies know you're officially on the market, and get your response ready.

Finally – and this is important advice – take ten long deep breaths before you go in to the meeting room. This will keep you calmer and more clear-headed. Honestly, it really works.

Face to Face with the Hatchet Man

If you genuinely want to leave, or most of your colleagues are getting the boot along with you, then none of the rest of this chapter is relevant. In this case, you need to ask three questions: Where's my cheque? Where do I sign? Can I leave now?

It's different when you don't want to go, and, even worse, you are one of only a few getting the sack, or, even worse still, the only one. Oh yes, it hurts. It's a shock. How you respond in the meeting, however, depends on whether or not the decision to make you redundant was about:

A   a genuine business need, which means that the decision really is nothing personal, or

B   a personal grievance.

A: It's Nothing Personal: Your Job Is Simply No Longer Required

If you are still within your probationary period, in your first year of employment at the company, or your contract is up, there is nothing you can do about it, unless you have hard evidence of unfair treatment. However, it is always worth carrying out a search on your legal rights. Every country is different when it comes to the law on making someone redundant, and there are always circumstances that may work in your favour. So at the very least take a little time to check out the law and industrial relations acts, either online or from a friendly HR or legal eagle. Try www.citizensinformation.ie/categories/employment/unemployment-and-redundancy/.

I know it's an obvious point, but in this instance, if you react in any way aggressively, your manager will immediately stop thinking about the awful thing he's doing and think only about how awful you are (and indeed will begin to feel somewhat happy about what he's doing). Nor will he act as a referee (but who cares, anyway: Joyce the cleaner has offered and has been accepted). No, just be calm and professional, and leave them with a positive impression, in case another job opportunity arises later on. This is sometimes difficult, particularly if you are surprised by the decision and are feeling a little blindsided.

So here are some tips which could make this difficult meeting a little easier to endure as you take your ten deep breaths, enter the room and take your seat.

1. MAKE THE JOKE THEY'VE ALREADY HEARD A HUNDRED TIMES

You know it: it's the hilarious glass-of-water-on-the-table joke. Ready?

'I hope that's gin.'

Haa haa haa. No, of course it's not funny. What's funny is that they are morally obliged to laugh uproariously at this, and any other stupid joke you might make. Make 'em suffer. Say it again. 'No really, I hope it really is gin.' Haa haa. Hours of fun. By the way, if there's no water for you on the table, ask for some and then make the joke.

2. ASK QUESTIONS . . . LOTS OF THEM

A regret some people have during the redundancy process is not asking enough questions (or *any* questions, in some cases). Feeling a little blindsided is normal, but it can cause you to leave without fully understanding why it was you and not other people who were chosen for the chop. And it's too late to wonder after the meeting. What may happen instead is that you turn things over and over in your head as you try to fill the gaps in your information. And this is a bad thing for you to do. You may end up thinking the worst about what was probably a fair and reasonable decision. And most managers (provided there is nothing personal in their decision) are more than happy to answer any questions you may have. The most important thing for you to remember is to be polite and respectful in your questioning.

Also, for your own peace of mind, it is important for you to know that they followed fair process and procedure in reaching their decision. If not, it will become obvious in the course of your questioning. So ask whatever questions you have in mind. The great thing about this is . . . they have to answer them!

Can't think of any questions? Here are a few:

So, after they have explained in great detail the whole process, the business strategy and why your role was made redundant, just shake your head and say:

A   'I don't understand . . . can you explain that to me again?'

(A little cheeky, because they may not remember what they have just said!)

B   Can I see the business strategy/sales figures/re-organisation document?

(If they have based the decision on any of the above documents, and refer to it in the course of the meeting, then you may be entitled to see them.)

C   What's going to happen to my responsibility to do X, Y and Z?

D   So what's going to happen to the team going forward? What will their priorities be?

(With C and D, you're looking for anything that will require even a part of your job specification. Which takes you on to the next question.)

E   So if you need to focus on X, Y and Z, surely you are going to need someone to do A, B and C?

If they start getting irritated, calmly explain that the redundancy has shattered your livelihood or career aspirations, or both, and that you, as an intelligent and capable individual, need to understand fully why you, and not others, were chosen. And it is equally important to make them realise that they would be just as devastated if it happened to them.

3. TAKE NOTES

The reason you should take notes is to do with the post-mortem you will obviously do. During the emotional roller coaster of the redundancy meeting, it is easy to forget what was said or, worse, to remember incorrectly. If you have notes from the meeting, you can conduct a calm review of it in the privacy of your own home and then make an informed decision on whether or not the decision was right and fair. This will help you move forward with wisdom, not emotion or, worse, paranoia.

4. END THE MEETING WELL

You won't want to, I know. But do. After you've made them explain the process/strategy/reasons really slowly ten times, asked a hundred irrelevant questions and made your quotient of stupid jokes, it's time to pack that spotty handkerchief and clear out. *Do it with dignity.* Stand up. Smile. Shake their hand. Tell them nicely that you'll keep in touch, and wish them luck. After all, the Hatchet Man has a man upstairs too! And more importantly, you never know what opportunities tomorrow might bring. I am constantly amazed at the number of people let go by their organisation who, a short time later, find their way back in. It could be you!

5. LEAVE THE BUILDING IMMEDIATELY

Say your goodbyes to people as you leave but do not stop for any longer than is needed for you to say (quickly) how sorry you are to be leaving, how much you will miss the people/the job/the perks. Those who really care will get in touch with you. Don't stop just to satisfy anyone else's curiosity or look for sympathy. It will leave you feeling worse. You need that last impression of you as you walk out the door to be positive, and the image of a downtrodden victim will not help. Under no circumstances should you go back to your desk unless you really, absolutely, have to (e.g. to collect your coat and bag). Get someone else to pick up whatever other stuff you've left. Go! Shoo!

If your redundancy comes with a future end date, then by all means return to your desk, but be ultra-discreet. Everything you say will be disseminated rapidly, so avoid the temptation to make your leaving any more stressful than it already is. Gossiping and bitching, unless it is with people you trust 100 percent, will damage you more than the person you are bitching about.

B: It's Personal!

If you are being let go because you did a terrible job within a reasonable time period, and they have evidence to prove it, don't waste another moment of your time. Take it on the chin, grab whatever they may give you, and go.

Of course, no one is ever going to admit that they are letting you go because they don't like the look of you, or because you wouldn't sleep with them, or because they intend to blame you for something that's about to blow, or take credit for your achievements. They are going to try and spin it so that it's nothing personal.

If, however, you know in your heart that the decision to let you go was personal, then the rules above still apply here. Below, however, are a few additional tips on how you could handle this particularly difficult meeting.

1. FUTURE-PROOF YOUR REPUTATION

The first thing you need to do during this type of dismissal is to hear from them how absolutely wonderful you are. This is important in case they decide to badmouth you after you've gone. You will then be able *honestly* to tell everyone how brilliant you are, using direct quotes from them as proof.

It will not be in their interests to indicate that your dismissal is something to do with your performance, as then they have to prove that this is the case. It's a potential legal landmine, unless they have hard evidence and have followed fair process in arriving at the decision.

If they don't have any real evidence of poor performance and it's really about a personal grievance, most managers have more savvy than to raise the subject of performance at all. In fact, they will go out of their way to avoid the subject. Also, with regard to bad-mouthing, remember that there are laws prohibiting slander, and if they (and you!) are smart, both sides will watch their words carefully.

So with this in mind, and knowing that they have no issues with your performance, look them in the eye and ask sincerely if your dismissal has anything to do with your work. (*'Of course not'*, the smart ones will say.) Then pick your biggest achievements (new contracts, new products, new processes, cost savings), and ask them if it had anything to do with that. (*'Absolutely not. A, B and C would never have happened if it hadn't been for you.'*) Push them gently until they are positively gushing about every single thing you ever touched. At this point, get a commitment that they will provide a reference in relation those achievements.

Then, after you have extracted these compliments and the commitment of a reference, tell them that you agree with everything they've said, because you *and others* also feel that you did an excellent job. Remind them of compliments that have been given to you by others. Remind them that you, too, have supporters – plenty of them. Make them realise that there will be risks involved in bad-mouthing you: it may rile your supporters, and come back to haunt them.

While justice is never guaranteed, all of this should help at least to minimise any future damage to your reputation when you are not there to defend yourself.

2. COME CLEAN ABOUT YOUR MISTREATMENT

If you are being downgraded or forced into a job you don't want, and your manager retains influence over your career, you may need to think twice about doing this. However, if he or she will have no influence over you and has genuinely treated you badly, not just in letting you go but prior to this, let him or her know. Don't just shrug and walk away, thinking that it would be better for you to say nothing. It's not; it's only better for your boss. He'll just think he's got clean away with it. You will be left reeling and will regret it later. I have heard this from quite a few people who found themselves in this situation. Their biggest regret was not confronting their manager or raising awareness of the problem when they had an opportunity to do so.

Common sense dictates that if your boss has acted unfairly or inappropriately, the first time he and everyone else hears this should *not* be in the exit meeting. You should have already highlighted the problem and sought to find a resolution. Otherwise, it smells of sour grapes and you would be advised to say nothing. Sadly, they will tend not to believe you anyway.

So, if the problem had already been highlighted to him and no resolution had been found, raise it again. Calmly and clearly, ask why he, for example:

treated you differently from others (and give examples)

treated you inappropriately (with examples)

did not fulfil agreed commitments

did not provide you with support that was provided to others (again, have some examples ready)

Let him know that his behaviour was unacceptable. Remind all of them sitting there that you had already highlighted the problem but that no resolution had been found. Tell him or her also that you had taken the job in good faith and had applied yourself conscientiously. In doing so, you expected to be treated in the same way as others. Remind him of the wonderful things he said about you earlier. Tell him how great you are. Make him feel like the biggest toad in the world. Which he is. Make him wonder what others, including his own boss, will think about what you've just said.

You may also consider arranging an exit meeting with HR to discuss the issue formally, or perhaps writing a formal complaint to his boss. It probably won't cause the manager any real grief, but it helps to know that others are now aware of his behaviour.

3. STAY CALM AND PROFESSIONAL

Tempted and justified as you may feel, losing your temper or crying will only make everyone forget about how horrible your boss is – and that's not what you want. You don't want the only topic of conversation to be you losing your temper, or having a hysterical crying fit, or threatening your boss. You've lost not only your job but your dignity, and you will feel weak and stupid later. Don't let them reduce you to that. And, in this instance, it is not required to shake his or her hand on the way out.

4. DO NOT THREATEN TO SUE OR RUSH INTO ANY LEGAL ACTION

If you feel you have a case, don't ruin it by telling them this too early. Wait until you have gathered your

incriminating evidence. Then get legal advice. Most solicitors worth their salt will tell you to leave it, learn from
it and move on. But this obviously depends on the hard
evidence you have gathered. Some new 'redundees' I
have spoken to took comfort from a single action, such
as sending a solicitor's letter seeking clarification on a
particular issue, and often find an acceptable resolution
after doing this. But generally speaking, moving forward
in wisdom is the best approach to take.

Top Tips on Surviving the Meeting

When It's Simply a Numbers Game

Take ten deep breaths as you enter the room. It
will keep you calm (as will over-dosing on Dr
Bach's Rescue Remedy, which I also recommend)

Make lots of irrelevant silly jokes – they are
morally obliged to laugh.

Ask lots of questions. It will save you hours of
mental head-wrecking later as you try to fill the
gaps in your knowledge.

Take notes. Relying on memory alone during this
emotional time is dangerous. Your imagination
will go into overdrive.

End the meeting well. Difficult as this may be.

Leave them with a positive impression. You never
know what opportunity tomorrow will bring.

Leave immediately. Don't wait around just to
satisfy everyone else's curiosity or promote
yourself as a victim.

5. THINK TWICE ABOUT RETALIATING

This is a thorny one. Some do, but most say that you should *never* do this: it may backfire and undermine you as much as the person you're targeting. To a large extent, I agree with this advice: most injustices should be treated as a valuable lesson learned. However, from listening to the terrible experiences suffered by some, it could be argued that losing your job or career path because of a personal issue with your boss could be one of those exceptions. If taking a stand against an injustice is important in helping you to move on (and if no one can talk you out of this course of action), then perhaps it could be the right thing for you. Discretion has its place more often, but perhaps so too does opening a small can of retaliation.

WHEN IT'S PERSONAL

Future-proof your reputation. In this day and age, our reps are all we've got, so guard it well.

Come clean about your mistreatment. If, of-course, you had already highlighted the problem and sought a resolution. If not, say nothing. No one will believe you anyway.

Stay calm and professional. Difficult as this may be. Don't let the stupidity of others reduce you to being a screamer or wailer. You're better than that.

Don't threaten to take legal action. Get advice first.

Think twice about retaliation. Success is the best revenge.

The Immediate Aftermath

1. Don't Try to Push Your Way Back In

The only exception to this rule is if your redundancy was about a business need but an opportunity has genuinely arisen. Then absolutely, jump on it before someone else does!

As a general rule, though, if no opportunity presents itself, don't hang around trying to push yourself back in the door – as a consultant, contractor or cleaner. Desperation is always a huge turn-off. You're out now; stay out. Don't keep 'dropping by' to say hello, to codge a free lunch, and so on. You'll only look more like an abandoned dog with no home to go to than the competent professional you know you are. If opportunities crop up, email and phone will suffice. They know where you are.

When it comes to post-redundancy visibility, less is definitely more.

2. Meet Only a Very Small Group of Your Ex-colleagues

Two. Three. At an absolute stretch, four. You don't want your aftermath to turn into a circus. You'll look less of a ringleader and more of a clown.

3. Don't Pressure Your Ex-colleagues to Do Anything for You

Whether that is to give you information, complain to the boss, or find you a job, don't corner them with demands too quickly. If they want to do any of these things, they will anyway. Real friends will naturally start thinking about ways to help you out, but putting too much pressure on them tends to make them not want to do those things – or see you again . . . ever.

4. TAKE EVERYTHING THAT'S ON OFFER

Sign up for any type of post-redundancy initiatives, be it career assessment, use of office facilities, counselling or further training. Swallow your pride and take full advantage of anything they have to offer. Why wouldn't you? I was amazed at the number of people who did not attend workshops or further training provided by the company because they were so angry (and perhaps still a little in denial). Wrong approach. Take *everything* they offer.

5. DON'T PRETEND TO BE HAPPY

Everyone sees through that and, believe it or not, it actually doesn't help, particularly if you're hoping that your friends will help sort you out. They'll be less inclined to help you if you're waxing lyrical about the joys of being unemployed. What you should try to be is honest and strong. Honest about how frustrated and let-down you feel, and strong in your determination that this is not going to deter you in any way. You know you're good. You *are* good! And those who know you, know that.

6. TALK ABOUT IT

Get your thoughts and feelings out there as soon as you can. Don't bottle it in. It's not healthy. And nor is it a sign of weakness. Your close friends and family have a fair idea of what's going on anyway, so you may as well tell them. Use your close friends as unpaid therapists. They won't mind – for a short while, anyway.

I'm emphasising the word 'close' here. It is crucial to trust your confidants implicitly. If you think that they might gossip or may not care, don't confide in them. Act strong and positive instead.

If you're talking to your colleagues, keep things short and simple. Relay back the positive aspects of the conversation with your boss: the good things he said about you, for instance. This has a number of effects but it can also create paranoia in your colleagues: 'If he can do this to a great person like X, then he can do it to me!' Staff being badly treated tends to affect the morale of others, and turnover of key staff can happen quite quickly afterwards.

TOP TIPS ON SURVIVING THE IMMEDIATE AFTERMATH

Don't try to push your way back in if an opportunity does not present itself. Desperation is a turn-off.

Stay away. When it comes to post-redundancy visibility, less is more.

Make a date to see only a very small selection of your ex-colleagues. Two or three – four max.

Relay the positive aspects only of the redundancy conversations.

Don't dwell on the negative. You are now all about your image.

Don't pressure your ex-colleagues to do anything. If they want to help, they will anyway.

Take everything on offer. Everything, even counselling.

Talk about it only to those you trust 100 percent.

Say nothing to those you don't trust.

Don't pretend to be happy. People understand that what you're going through is tough.

3

You're Out!

Welcome to a New World

The typical redundancy cycle generally runs as follows:

shock, denial, anger, depression, acceptance.

In reality, the cycle is a little more complicated than that. I would characterise it as:

PHASE 1 (0–2 WEEKS)

Anger, denial, worry, shock, jealousy, acceptance

PHASE 2 (1–4 WEEKS)

Sense of hope, sense of urgency, cheerfulness, confidence

PHASE 3 (4 WEEKS+, WITH NO OPPORTUNITY IN SIGHT)

Panic, anxiety, anger, low confidence, loneliness, feeling defeated

PHASE 4 (WHEN THE NEW OPPORTUNITY FINALLY ARRIVES)

Relief, feelings of 'having survived' and of having gained in strength and wisdom, forgiveness, nervousness (regarding the new opportunity)

In addition, people's individual reaction to redundancy and forced unemployment is dependent on the following factors:

1. How long have you been out there looking for a job?

2. Were you the only one, or one of only a few, in the team to be made redundant?

3 Did you want to leave?

If you wanted to leave, the over-riding emotion tends to be relief, sometimes tinged with a little worry.

When everyone's going, there tends be a short cycle of the typical emotions mentioned above – anger, sadness, acceptance – but there's always comfort and security in numbers.

When you're singled out, it's horrible. Concurrent feelings of shock, resentment, denial, happiness, calm acceptance, even relief, can sweep over you . . . even while you're still in the meeting! The unfortunate thing here is that this roller coaster of emotions will stay with you until you find another, or better, job. You'll have good days, bad days and terrible days as you struggle to find a better place. If you're lucky, it won't last too long. If you're not, you need to be determined not to let your anxiety put you in a negative frame of mind. You don't want to become your own worst enemy. Later on, I have some tips to help you to remain positive in this situation.

Who Suffers More?

I have noticed that individuals who suffer more from the negative effects of redundancy and unemployment tend to be:

1. THOSE HIGHER UP THE FOOD CHAIN

This is probably due to their level of visibility, but much of it is also a result of their natural feeling that someone as experienced and competent as them should never have to suffer the ignominy of being cast aside. It is also undoubtedly due to the small pool of opportunities that exist at this level. When you're young and relatively inexperienced, what you do in the interim is not going to matter too much, but the same thing certainly matters to those who have reached a senior level. They can't 'take anything' or temp without the risk of damaging their credibility. This may not be the case in the US or Asia where if you don't work, you don't eat, or for immigrants, for whom it is generally acceptable to do a job in the host country they would never have done at home.

2. THE SOCIALLY CHALLENGED

Social and interpersonal skills are probably the most important skills we have when it comes to getting a job and keeping it. When you aren't blessed with an approachable manner and a positive attitude, you can quickly find yourself isolated. And when you're unemployed and spending a lot of time alone, isolation can make you crazy. So with no specific place to go, socially challenged, angry or shy types tend to sink into a hole. This is quite a serious handicap, particularly when you consider the importance of 'networks' in getting you back on your feet. Recovery can require a 'fake it 'til you make it' approach, or a complete change of attitude. You don't want to become your own worst enemy. Later on, I have some tips for people who find it hard to get out there and for those who are distracted by negative thinking.

3. THE PROUD

This refers to people who could be starving but will still smile broadly and say 'fantastic' when asked how things are going. The quickest road to destruction, my friends. There is no weakness in admitting that you are not where you want to be and need a helping hand. Nobody minds helping good, talented people who made a wrong turn or just got in with the wrong people. In fact, they will be happy to be of assistance – if they can. Let them know you're in need.

4. THE OUTRAGED

When you have experienced something awful like losing your job, the easiest thing to do is to turn it over and over in your head, which can eventually lead to paranoia and depression. But reliving the trauma will only serve to make you madder and crazier. And you're wasting valuable energy that should be spent getting back out there. Stop thinking and get moving.

5. THE LONG-TERMERS

It's relatively easy to remain buoyed up and confident when you're out of a job for a short time and fairly sure that an opportunity is close at hand. Real strength, maturity and resilience comes in when you can't see anything on the horizon and the weeks start turning into months, even years. This is the time when demons will surface and haunt you. For long-termers, it is not just about managing what's going on in the outside world but, more importantly, managing the demons that lurk inside. You're vulnerable at this stage, so you don't want to indulge in any kind of destructive thinking which threatens your self-belief or positive outlook. *It will work out. Don't even think about giving up.*

6. THE FINANCIALLY BURDENED

This goes without saying. Their worry and despair peels off them in strips. Later on, I have some tips on getting and saving money. It is important to know that plenty of working people have equal or bigger financial problems.

7. AGED FORTY-FIVE+

Let's face it, in job-land, forty-five is considered old. If you've managed to secure a manager's post before that time, fine, but otherwise it's not nice to be forty-five-plus and looking for the same job as a twenty-five-year-old. The point here, as with all hang-ups, is that if you think age is an issue, it will become one. If you don't, then it won't. In every team I have worked in, there was always a wide range of age groups, and I can never, ever, remember anyone worrying about this fact. The truth is that, unless you're doddery, half-deaf and pushing a Zimmer frame around, age is of no relevance to anyone . . . particularly now in the age of hair dye and botox! A positive attitude, good character and energy goes much further.

Surviving the Forty-eight-hour Aftermath

So you're out. No job. No prospects of a job this side of Christmas. And it's September. Your future looms before you, dark and uncertain. So, without wishing to sound like we're in a Keanu Reeves movie . . . what do you do? What *do* you do?

1. BREATHE. LAUGH. BREATHE. LAUGH.

Remember, you're not dying! There is a job out there for you. And it's closer to you than you think. Maybe it's a temporary position until the tide turns. Maybe it's your dream job. Maybe it's an OK job with less money or responsibility or perhaps in the physical location you wish to be in. Remember, there are over ten times more people working than not working. Ten times! There *are* jobs out there, even in the worst economic circumstances. There is an old business saying that goes: 'Never worry about the business outlook. Always be on the lookout for business.' This is true for you too. When these workers emigrate, die, get promoted or go on leave, who's going to replace them?

So take ten long, deep breaths every time you feel anxious, and laugh. At yourself. At *Tom & Jerry.* At any funny story you hear. Laugh. Laugh and then laugh some more. And when there's nothing going on to make you laugh, invent it. Think of your school days or your kids. Laugh yourself into a stupor. And breathe deep some more. (I'm serious about the deep-breathing thing: it really helps to calm a worried mind.)

Why laugh? Surely, if anything, you should be crying, raging? Why? Because laughter really is the best medicine in the fight against depression, and the bottom line is that we all take ourselves way, *way* too seriously! So you've no paid job? So what? You'll get one. And that goes for anyone, of any age, with any number of mouths to feed. And yes, it gets more difficult to laugh as the months wear on and the debts mount up, but then undoubtedly it becomes more important to do so too!

You will come back stronger. Do not doubt yourself for one second! You are a better, wiser person now than you have ever been.

In fact, this rule is so important that I have a good mind to add it to every single rule in this book.

2. GET OUT OF THE HOUSE!

Sounds strange, but a break of any kind at this point will help you in unimaginable ways. If you can afford it, leave the country. If not, book yourself and family into a friend's house, or your parents' house, or a B&B along a pretty stretch of coastline. Give yourself one day minimum and three days maximum. That's all. This break is your period of reflection (and ranting to anyone who is stupid enough to sit within a hundred metres of you). You will also want to ask yourself some tough questions. What do I do now? Do I want to continue with this career? Should I have played the game better? Was I to blame?

Well, the answers to all of the above are obvious. Yes, you'll be absolutely fine. You will find another job. Perhaps you were to blame or maybe you were not. In the end, you probably had only a small part to play in creating the situation you're now in, so don't beat yourself up about it too much. Unless you acted the goat and did a really terrible job, much of your situation is actually more to do with other people and other things. And you will undoubtedly have learned from the experience. All you have to do is read the life stories of some the most successful people on our planet. Many of them overcame incredible obstacles and endured multiple disappointments before everything came together for them – in their forties (boxer George Foreman) and fifties (US President Abraham Lincoln), their sixties (home and garden guru Martha Stewart) or even their eighties (American painter Anna Roberts, aka 'Grandma Moses')!

Remember: there is always time for a comeback.

Anyway, the break is your way of coming to terms with all of the above. Going home is the natural end point. And I will repeat that: the end point.

The second reason for getting away is not to use your own home for this phase. Otherwise, you'll find it impossible to disassociate your house from this negative period. It's interesting to hear of the number of people who, when forced to stay at home for long periods of time, end up hating their homes, even moving when they got back on track. An expensive and time-consuming exorcism! For me, I went down the cheaper road of redecoration.

Even if you have job opportunities lined up, take a break anyway. It's good to use breaks like this to take a sneaky holiday: we don't get the opportunity to do this very often.

3. DECIDE ON A SHORT-TERM PLAN OF ACTION

The real output of this period of reflection, however, is to come home with a clear plan of action. There may be things that you would not consider as a long-term choice, but faced with unemployment, and with the urgent objective of getting back into a work routine, you should also consider roles that are even vaguely related to what you do – or used to do. And it doesn't stop there. The plan needs to specify:

What exactly are you willing to do? From dream job to desperate. Lay it down. What is it?

Will you be able to do this? Will you need further training?

Who do you need to contact?

This way you come home focused and clear-headed.

TIPS ON SURVIVNG THE FORTY-EIGHT-HOUR AFTERMATH

Breathe. Laugh. Breathe. Laugh. Know that worse things happen.

Believe that you will come back stronger. You will.

Get out of the house for a few days' reflection and to figure out a short-term plan. Take one day minimum.

Return home positive. Don't let the demons of anger and fear enter your home. Leave them elsewhere.

Don't beat yourself up. Job loss is mostly about circumstances beyond our control.

Get a short-term plan. What am I willing to do for the next three months? How can I make this happen? Who will I call?

The Unique World of the Unemployee

Every circumstance we encounter informs and colours our view of the world, for better or for worse. Redundancy and unemployment is no different. Our lives change, our time is spent differently, and our perception of the world is, at least temporarily, altered. This happens as soon as you hear the news. The people across the table telling you the news will somehow look weird to you, and you'll start to notice strange things about them – such as they way they sit, their accent, the mole on their forehead, their immaculate nail grooming. Even the environment, the same old light flooding in through the office window, the train journey home, the woman in the bakery beside your house, everything and every-body seems different. Why do we feel different? What is this experience called? – Well, it's called being an 'outsider' and it's a weird, lonely feeling indeed.

This altered reality even includes how we look at our day. And believe it or not, there are some unexpected pleasures to be had there.

How the Day Looks to an Unemployee

BEST TIMES OF THE DAY

EARLY MORNING

Nothing gives you more pleasure than being able to take your time in the morning, enjoy your coffee, read the paper and wave your spouse or flatmates off as they face a frustrating journey to work through the terrible grid-lock. That hour before 9.30 AM is a nice one. Savour it. When you go back to full-time work, you'll daydream about it!

MID-MORNING

If you've had a really good run of things, that is. You managed to talk to a few important people, get some good advice – and some good feedback on a recent job application. You feel like you've earned that cup of coffee and crossword puzzle.

WORST TIMES OF THE DAY

MID-MORNING

When you realise you've wasted two and a half hours on God-knows-what and still haven't checked one thing off your list. Irritating!

LATE AFTERNOON/EARLY EVENING

When you know that the hope you had in the morning that something good would come out of the day is starting to fade and that soon your housemates or partner or neighbours will be home from their day's work. You know they're going to ask you if you found a job . . . and you're going to have to say no. Not nice!

A Typical Week for an Unemployee

SUNDAY

Nice. You can relax and enjoy it, have a drink or two at dinner without being concerned about the fact that you may feel groggy in the morning. No worrying about that meeting or project, or that annoying colleague with the loud voice. And you can enjoy a late-night movie knowing that it doesn't matter if you're tired the next day. You don't have to be anywhere! Yippee! You can even leave your ironing in a heap. You can do it any day of the week (But don't – it's quite depressing to pass it by sixteen times a day!)

MONDAY

A great day to be unemployed! While everyone else drags themselves off to work through the horrendous Monday-morning traffic, wishing they could be anywhere else doing anything else, you can wave them off, cosy up on the sofa, enjoy your coffee and read the Sunday papers with the guilty pleasure of knowing you don't have to do anything too taxing, or be anywhere at all. Because, to be honest, no one wants to hear from you before 10 AM on a Monday morning anyway; they will actually resent you if they do! In the misery of unemployment, Mondays are an unexpected pleasure.

TUESDAY

Tuesday is OK. The week is young enough that you can still have hope. Hope that this week 'It's all gonna happen' – you're going to get that call! You're back to your early morning office routine, still enthusiastic, hopeful and full of energy.

WEDNESDAY

A bit scary. It's that midweek crisis that tells you that while you know you're not yet beaten, it feels as though you are. You mull over the last few days with an emptiness that comes from lack of achievement and start asking yourself big questions like 'Is this it?', 'Is this what it's going to be like for the rest of the week?', 'Why am I here?', 'Would anyone miss me if I was gone?'

THURSDAY

The autumn of your week, when the action lists are ticked off (you *are* making those lists, aren't you?), possibilities start fading and you know the good days are over. The difference is that you don't care as much as you did yesterday. It's late-night shopping/pub night/ cinema night, and you have people to see and things to do – even if it's just renting a DVD and talking to your best friends on the telephone. You've accepted the week as being what it is (a complete f****** write-off!), and you're calm, almost philosophical, about it.

FRIDAY

The last stand. You don't want the week to be over. Hell, it's only just begun for you. You have some new ideas. You scramble to salvage the remains of the possibilities you thought you had, clinging on to any flicker of life, gasping for the last breath that remains of the week, furiously making plans that next week will be different. Next week – when it's *all* going to happen. All fired up and then . . . 4 PM arrives . . . no one's taking your calls . . . it's time to be still . . . to stop resisting the inevitable and admit defeat. You're still unemployed!

Friday evening is a strange one. You've nothing to celebrate, and you don't have the satisfaction of feeling that you've 'earned' the weekend. Friday evenings are always the times when I used to feel really out of sync with the working world – out of sync with that 'Friday feeling'.

SATURDAY

Good. You can't look for a job, so you have to focus on other things. Your partner, friends or housemates are now home – so you have people to play with and pretend you're like the rest of the working world, just going about your business, doing your shopping, picking up DVDs, mowing the lawn, and so on.

Saturday evenings are always a bit hairy. You can't go wild and blow off steam. Apart from having no steam to blow off, you've had no fuel to make the steam in the first place. This is my long-winded way of saying that you're broke and you're going to have to manage on a curry chips and a DVD. If you're clever, you'll get yourself invited to events. But more about cheap ways to entertain yourself later.

BAD TIMES OF THE MONTH TO BE UNEMPLOYED

Payday. Don't torture yourself by meeting up with people on payday. It's a killer – especially when you have an overdraft of €3,000 in your bank account.

BEST TIMES OF THE MONTH TO BE UNEMPLOYED

Warm, sunny days and cold, rainy days . . . goes without saying.

4

Get Ready to Jump Back In

THE HARDEST WORK IS UNEMPLOYMENT – THE MINUTE YOU WAKE
UP IN THE MORNING YOU'RE ON THE JOB
SLAPPY WHITE (US COMIC)

Get Organised –
A Good Start is Half the Battle

This chapter is not really for those taking a short break from the workplace with the next opportunity already fixed up. If that is you, then lounging about reading dusty novels and watching old movies with a bottle of wine is exactly what you should be doing. If you're one of those people who has absolutely no clue how long you are going to be out of work, then you need to prepare yourself for a lot of re-adjustment, whether this is mastering the art of working from home, proactively selling yourself, or building and working your contacts network – or even just getting your ass out of bed! (It's harder than you realise!) And because a good start is half the battle, below are tips that have helped to get me back in the game.

Get Connected

Fact: networking and research are the most important things you can do for your career. Not brilliance. Not wit. Not education. You'd be amazed and depressed by the numbers of brilliant, witty, educated people who are out of a job. People do business with people they know, or have heard of or, even better, have heard from! So get connected with whatever communication tools you can think of. Accessibility is crucial. Most work-related communication is via email or phone, and most information you need is on the internet. Get hooked up to the internet and get a second phone into your 'office' (your mobile will suffice). Opportunities pass by so quickly, and if you're out of the communication loop, you'll miss out. If you're taking a few days off (which you are entitled to do, and don't be afraid to go away), then ensure that you leave an out-of-office message on your email or voicemail. Carry your mobile phone everywhere and leave it on. If you can afford it, invest in one of those mobile email devices, so you're always 'on' and always accessible. Make connecting and being accessible a priority.

Working From Home
How to Do It Successfully

There's a science to successful homeworking. Some people master it, some give in to the TV, the gardening, the ironing or the fridge on the first attempt. For me, it was the internet. (I was convinced that if I was connected to the internet, I was working.) So I really had to work at it. The single biggest adjustment for me was first to *believe* that I was 'at work'. It was weird to change my perception that my home was now my one and only work environment and – even weirder – that it required a certain amount of work ethic and work practice on my part to achieve anything I planned to do. That was hard. My home was my playground, my relaxation den. *Not* a workplace. Not a place where I acted professionally and responsibly. It took me a while to adjust, and in doing so, I wasted valuable time – which I regret. Below are some of the things that worked for me when it came to managing your work life from your home:

1. CREATE A WORK ROUTINE

Maintaing a work routine is a crucial psychological prop when you are unemployed. By maintaining what resembles a work schedule and normal working hours, you keep connected to the working world and are less inclined to feel like an outsider. This also helps you engage with the 'workers' on an equal footing – which will help your confidence.

2. MAKE A WORK SPACE IN YOUR HOME

Make a work space (even if it's a tiny corner of your bedroom) that resembles an office, complete with computer, plant, phone, address books, message boards, printer, files, folders and Post-its. This helps you avoid the useless practice of working in every room in the house to keep you triply inspired. It won't work. Build a work nest and settle there.

3. DON'T JUST SIT THERE: WORK!

Two things are important here:

A. *Get up early!* There's an old saying: 'If you lose an hour in the morning, you'll spend all day looking for it.' This is so true. So, be at your 'office' by 8.30 to 9 AM every day. (You've no traffic to wade through!) Even if it's to check your mails quickly, look at websites or draw up a list of people to call – be there! At that time. As you would in any job. And just like in any other job, turn your computer off at a set time each day. Dipping in and out of it day, evening and night will mean that, psychologically, you will never get away from it. You absolutely need to, even just to preserve your sanity!

I'm serious about getting up early. It is depressing to stagger out of bed at midday, groggy and bored. In psychological terms, the day is wasted, and anything that needs to be done gets pushed on to another day, simply because you wasted the morning hours. I don't know why this is true, but it is!

B: *Act industrious while sitting in this area.* This is really hard to achieve when all you want to do is play computer games, Google your ex-colleagues and gaze at your distorted self in the back of a spoon, but it's extremely important for maintaining your sense of purpose. So that means you need to do the following:

1. *Have something planned to do there.* Moping and staring at the screen is not allowed. Otherwise, leave it.

2. *Don't wear your pyjamas* unless you are one of the few people who can genuinely work well in their pyjamas. Don't fool yourself, like I did.

3. *Shower and dress first thing in the morning.* Wear your favourite work clothes and perfume or cologne. Looking good can make you feel good.

4. *Never use your 'office' as a place to feel sorry for yourself.* A place to gossip, yes, but hey, you are at work after all!

4. KEEP THE TV OFF!

Watching TV, your brain shuts down with alarming speed, and if you find a triple bill of John Wayne movies (you know who you are!) or a *Dallas* special, you're finished for the day. Better to turn on the radio if you're feeling lonely.

5. TAKE BREAKS – AND THE ODD LIBERTY

If you feel yourself getting down or bored, stand up and leave the 'office'. Have a coffee, buy a newspaper, call your friends, pull weeds from the garden. After all, forty-five minutes of enthusiastic, confident 'work' in your 'office' is better than hours of moping and time-wasting, which just makes you feel ten times worse come the end of the day. You may as well be on the golf course! There is no need to sit at the desk all day thinking you have to be there. You don't. There are only so many calls and CV and interview preps you can do. Two or three really productive hours a day is good.

Also, if you're not up to it some days, just take a 'sickie' or a sneaky half-day off to laze about. As you would in any job!!

6. MANAGE THE MINUTE-MUNCHERS

I don't know what it is about time at home, but I'm convinced that certain hours just don't exist. I can usually remember 8 to 10 AM. I remember because it is the time of the day when I loved having nowhere to go. But 10.30 AM to noon? . . . No. Neither does 3 to 4.58 PM ring a bell. The last two minutes before 5 PM – oh yes, that's normally when I race to the post office or bank, or make frantic calls I should have made during the day but somehow didn't get round to. So be extra-viligant about those pesky minute munchers – they'll creep up on you and eat up your entire day before you can say: 'I'll just see what's on after *Oprah* . . . it might be educational.'

6. MAKE LISTS, AND FOLLOW THEM

The day before, make a list of everything you should do (including the small things), and the next day, do them! Just like you do in any job. Hold yourself accountable. Tick off what you've done and write yourself a daily progress report. When you write down the 'work' you did, and it's interesting how quickly you'll start to compete with yourself, or hang your head in shame! Either way, it will make an impact.

It's amazing how incapacitated you become when you don't have external instructions on what to do each day. With no deadlines, your brain and sense of responsibility can shut down within a few weeks! I lost count of the number of times I planned to do simple things, like pay bills, call people, do certain jobs or walk a hundred metres down the road to post letters – and never got round to it until two minutes to closing time! Until I wrote it down, with a time limit attached, and made a deal with myself to do it first thing. So think of yourself as a budding entrepreneur and write those lists. They scream: 'Get out of that bed, you lazy lump, and start working.'

7. BASE YOUR DAY AROUND ENJOYABLE THINGS

When you focus on a boring or uncomfortable task, de-motivation will set in. In other words, you are less likely to do it – or anything else, for that matter. If, on the other hand, you say to yourself 'I will leave here on the dot of 2 PM today to play a round of golf/join a friend for coffee/go for a massage', the positive feeling surrounding looking forward to this activity will help motivate you to do the boring tasks before you go, like applying for jobs, or uncomfortable things, like calling a contact to ask for help. This really works: remember how productive you are at work in the week leading up to your holidays? So have something enjoyable to look forward to every day, and you'll get much more done.

TOP TIPS FOR WORKING FROM HOME

Maintain a work routine. It is your lifeline to the working world.

Create a space in your home which resembles work.

Get up early. Lose an hour in the morning and you'll spend all day looking for it.

Don't just sit there: work! Work through your lists, your contact book, whatever it is you planned to do.

Act industrious when in your office. Dress the part, act the part, and have something planned to do.

Take the odd liberty or sickie. Just like you would in a real job.

Keep the TV off even if you hear it calling your name. Turn on the radio to drown out the roar.

Watch out for those minute-munchers. They'll chew up your day faster than a *Dallas* special.

Draw up lists of things to do and follow them. What you can measure, you can manage!

Base your day around enjoyable things. You'll feel more motivated and will do more.

5

Get Out There

The Job Won't Come to You

There's no magic to getting a job, and no, the world is not actually against you. It just seems like that when you're on the outside. However, it *is* true that some people appear to breeze from one opportunity to another, whereas others seem stuck in a dark hole. Having been both types – and observed them in others – I can tell you that there is a marked difference in the approach taken by both of them.

The starting point here is to accept the fact that it is not enough to *half-do* it. When it comes to getting the job you want, a *full-on* and *sustained* effort is required. Nothing else will work. Trust me: I tried the half-baked approach, and it gets you a half-baked response and a half-baked job, if you're lucky.

Everybody has their tricks when it comes to getting a job. Here are some of mine.

Don't Talk: Mobilise

I've mentioned this before, and I'm going to say it again and again. In these times of uncertainty, there is only one surefire way of getting yourself a job: *talk to people.*

Network. Connect. Looking for a job without letting the world know what you're doing is, to quote a phrase, like winking in the dark. You know you're doing it, but no one else does.

This chapter may not matter if there are oodles of jobs out there and just one call will get you in (yes, there were days like that – I treasure the memories!), or perhaps you're so experienced that people are calling you. But in general, unless you like depressing yourself waiting for the phone to ring, you have little choice but to swallow your pride, pick up the phone and 'work' your network – however small it may be.

This may sound weird, but for some reason, I didn't really grasp this reality until I was into my third month of unemployment. Yes, I'd let people know I was looking for a job, but I'd never really 'worked' them. Maybe it was stupid pride, naivety or an inflated sense of my own ability to get any job I wanted on my own. Maybe it was a female thing: I do believe that networking generally comes easier for men than women. Or more worryingly, maybe it was that I was too focused on *activity* ('Well, I did call three people today, good job me!') and not enough on *results* ('But nobody had anything suitable for me. Oh well, at least I tried.')

I woke up from that dream eventually! I was getting nowhere with the agencies, who only wanted technical or sales people, and the big career clock was ticking away. It was, to put it mildly, depressing. So, without starting to sound like Dr Phil (who had become my new best friend, thanks to the quality time I was spending watching daytime TV), I got real and got talking to my contacts again – this time with a more focused approach.

I didn't always get it right and made all the usual mistakes: over-demanded from one and nearly lost him as a friend; sulked if people brushed me off; got upset when others didn't return my mails *immediately* (telling myself that I would have gotten back to them straight away if they had mailed *me*); bored people with my sob stories; or didn't really get to the point quickly enough and lost their interest.

But I think the biggest mistake people make is not believing in themselves enough, and letting it show!

Tips on Working Your Contact Network

1. WRITE A CONTACT LIST

Of all the people, and their contact details, who could potentially help you. Make sure they're over the age of twenty-one. (Tempting though it may be to hand out your CV at your nephew's Communion mass, it's just not right! OK, maybe I gave one or two people my phone number *after* the mass, but that's all!) When you've drawn up the list, prioritise:

A   Who do I need to call urgently?

B   Who do I need to call if the urgent list generates nothing?

C   Who will I need to call when the sheriff arrives to take away the TV?

2. INCLUDE WORK COLLEAGUES, EX-BOSSES, EX-COLLEGE MATES, FAMILY, RELATIVES, FRIENDS OF FRIENDS, GYM BUDDIES, THE BANK MANAGER . . . AND *THEIR* FRIENDS TOO!

You see where I'm going here! Get the word out there: a talented, experienced individual is looking for work. And don't listen to your mother when she tells you not to bother your uncles and aunts. You're *not* bothering them. You're telling them that you're unemployed and need to work, and are asking them to pass on your CV to a relevant contact. I have lost count of the number of fellow colleagues and graduates who have got their breaks from family connections. If you can ask strangers for help, you can – in fact, *should* – ask those closer to home. Mostly, they are happy to help.

3. DECIDE WHAT YOU WANT FROM THEM *BEFORE* YOU TALK TO THEM

No one will ever be able to help you if you're not clear about three things:

A   What you're really good at.

B   What you're willing to work at – from 'dream' to 'desperate'.

C   What you want them to do for you.

No one cares enough to figure all of this out on their own. And remember, don't insult people by sending a CV that is out of date or badly put together.

4. DON'T BE TOO PUSHY OR DEMANDING

A few friendly reminders tends to be all most people need – if they wish to help you. The sad truth is that most people, with the best will in the world, will not be in any position to help you directly. Don't badger them, put them in too awkward a position, or resent them if they are genuinely unable to help. Those who can help and want to, will. If, after a few reminders, they honestly can't, thank them for their interest, take their good wishes as sincere, and tell them you will keep in touch. Move on to the next person.

5. DON'T BE NEGATIVE

Much as you would like to pour your heart out about how tough your life is, don't. You'll scare people. Unless the person you're with is a very close friend or confidant, keep the sob stories to yourself. Be positive and hopeful.

6. ASK FOR REFERRALS

Remember the degrees-of-separation theory – and figure out what six people are standing between you and that big decision-maker. Ask for a recommendation or, better still, a personal introduction.

7. AS EARLY AS POSSIBLE, MAKE THE CALL TO THE CONTACT YOURSELF

Don't rely on your husband, mother or best friend to do all the introductory work, or the contact may think you're lazy, and expect the world to drop at your feet.

8. GET OUT AND SOCIALISE

Go to as many social gatherings as you can – small or large. I know that you won't want to, but trust me, it may be the most important thing you do. And make a point of *not once* mentioning your job search to anyone during these get-togethers. Give yourself – and everyone else – a much needed break from the subject. You'll be amazed the way opportunities crop up when the pressure's off.

9. BELIEVE IN YOURSELF

Remember your achievements and what it took to accomplish them. Believe that you are worthy of the best job out there. Believe that your circumstances are temporary and only marginally to do with you; that they do not reflect your capability – because they don't.

Top Tips on Working Your Contact Network

Create a list of your contacts from all aspects of your life: work, home and play. Opportunities can come from the strangest places.

Pick up that phone and get talking. Telepathy is only for the movies!

Prioritise those who need an urgent call, but don't forget the 'call only if desperate' list. You'll probably need it.

Decide what you want from them before you call: what you're good at, what you're willing to do, what you'd like them to do for you.

Send an up-to-date, well-put-together CV

Don't be too pushy or demanding. A few friendly reminders is usually all you need.

Don't be negative. Positivity is the only game in town when it comes to job-hunting.

Ask for referrals. Remember the degrees-of-separation theory.

Make as early an introduction as possible so that your contacts can see that you are a go-getter. Don't rely on others to sell you.

Socialise. Have fun. Enjoy yourself. It will show.

Believe in yourself. You then give others the chance to believe in you too.

'Work' the Recruitment Agencies

The same rules apply to working the agencies as working your network of personal contacts. However, meetings with recruitment agencies are different because, unlike your friends and relatives, the agents neither know nor care about you. These meetings should always be treated as round-one job interviews, even when there is no obvious job on the table.

So, apart from the obvious (i.e. shower, shave, dress smart, and be on time), there are a few other things you should remember:

1. BE POSITIVE WITHOUT OVERDOING IT

As I said before, believe in your strengths and abilities. Believe also that much of your current circumstances had little to do with you, so don't let them weigh you down. (Or if you do, never, ever let it show in public.) And don't say anything negative, no matter how tempted you may be. On the other hand, overdoing the positivity can be just as bad, by making you seem insincere or, worse, as though you are hiding something. Aim for a measured, calmly positive approach.

2. PREPARE IN ADVANCE

What do you want them to know about you? There are four important areas here:

   i.   Key achievements and strengths relevant to suitable roles;

   ii. Roles you would consider suitable in the immediate and short term;

   iii. If you are making a career change, have a good explanation as to why you are – and this does not include 'Because I tried X and it didn't work out' or 'It seems like it could be interesting'. These type of answers indicate that you're a quitter or don't really know what you want.

iv. Interesting things to help you stand out from the crowd, e.g. unusual hobbies, awards, instances where you've represented your country, academic achievements, and so on.

And always keep in mind what you want them to do for you: recommend you to employers, give you advice, set up client meetings. I cannot stress enough that if you don't (a) believe in yourself and (b) come to the meeting prepared, you are fighting a losing battle with the agencies.

The recruitment agencies: Are you feeling the love?

Lets talk honestly about handling these (sometimes) mad people. In my experience, I haven't always basked in the glow of their warm endorsement.

So I got to thinking, and realized that, while there was a lot of love out there, it was reserved for a certain type of job-hunter – I call them the 'streamliner'. They picked a career, trained extensively in that one career and stayed in the mould. Simple to categorise and easy to sell. Agencies scour the streets looking for a 'streamliner', because it represents money in the bank for them.

Me? No. *No*. Uh-uh. I am the type that makes sure the agency earns their fee. Getting someone like me a job is where they start paying . . . in sweat.

Now, that does not mean that I'm not bankable. *God* no! I *am*! It's just . . . well I'm what you'd call a 'broadstroker' – a 'sweeping generalist'.

I didn't mean for things to end up like that. I visualised things turning out very differently. ('Visualised', not 'planned! Apparently they're not the same thing!) But for me, life was a learning extravaganza. The more alternative, the more challenging, the situation, the better I believed that my experience would be. So in I jumped and just became whatever the situation demanded of me. And I did learn. About people – myself, mainly – in so many different environments, confronted with different challenges. I learned when to hold on, when to walk away and, to finish the cliché, when to run. I learned how to make things work when I really didn't have a clue, how to exploit the situation when I did, how to get people to believe in something when they didn't really care. Yes, I learned. But then, when I present my experienced and learned self to an agency, it always ends in tears (mine).

How the meeting tends to be for a 'broad-stroker'

Below is a snapshot of what it was like for a 'broad-stroker' like me when they were faced with those mad (but truly lovely) people in the recruitment agencies. (This actually happened.)

Long silence as the recruitment executive scans my CV, with furrowed brow, as we sit cramped in the smallest office in the building, where no tea or coffee is *ever* served.

HIM   *(Deep breath)* Riiiiiight . . . *(After what seems like five years)* OK. What . . . exactly . . . are you looking for? *(said with worried and slightly bemused smile)*

ME   (*Deep breath*) A manager's job, in the area of product development, business development,

70

training, as well as a bit of channel management, in any sector, technical, non-technical (*bigger breath*) . . . I've done it all.

HIM   Greeeeatt (*he says, completely unconvincingly*)

Long silence

HIM   I see you've done market research.

ME   Yes, when I left college (*ten years ago!*) to fill in the months until something better came along.

HIM   Riiiiight so, would you be interested in going back to it?

ME   What?

HIM   I can see you have some *excellent* market-research experience. (*For the record, my market-research experience received a mere footnote at the end of my packed-to-the-brim CV.*)

Open, raw laughter (on my part)

ME   Well, I wouldn't say 'excellent', and I wasn't exactly at the coalface. In fact, I hated market research, which is why I left. (*At this point, I'm noticing his strange, intense stare*)

HIM   I think you would be *excellent* at market research (*he almost screams*), and I have a good eye for these things.

ME   Really? . . . You do? . . . So what about the rest of my experience?

HIM   Mmm. Could be more difficult. Hard to know
        what you actually . . . *achieved.*

ME   OK, I see. Should I rewrite my CV?

HIM   *Great idea.* Now what you need to do is make the
        market-research side of it more prominent. Men-
        tion the clients you worked with and your role in
        helping *them* to succeed. *Your contribution.* What
        you brought to the table to maintain the prof-
        itability of your organisation. (*You should know,
        he's punching his closed fist at this stage!*) try and
        put some real figures round it, discuss the chal-
        lenges you faced, how YOU overcame the obsta-
        cles . . . where that company is today because of
        YOU . . . You know, the usual stuff (!!!).

ME   Well, I was actually talking about the rest of my
        experience, you know, the experience that makes
        up the first two pages and the last eight years
        because apart from hating market research,
        which I mentioned earlier, I really didn't do much
        in there, other than stuff envelopes, edit quest-
        ionnaires and badger old ladies to complete the
        questionnaires properly . . . which just broke my
        heart.

HIM   *Fantastic. Great.* That's all good stuff.

ME   No . . . it really wasn't . . . And as for what I did *for*
        the company. Well, I believe they closed the office
        down soon afterwards.

HIM   Well, greaaat, that's decided then, I'll put you
        forward for the market-research job.

ME   Is that a window? Greeeeaaaat, you wouldn't mind if I jumped out of it, would you?

How to get the best from agencies

1. CHOOSE THREE AGENCIES AT THE MOST

and develop a close working relationship with them, rather than making random attacks on one agency after

---

TOP TIPS ON GETTING THE AGENCIES TO 'SELL YOU' RATHER THAN 'HOLD YOU ON FILE'

See the tips on working your contact networks. Most are relevant to the agencies.

Come prepared. Bring an up-to-date CV and think about jobs you would consider, from 'dream' to 'desperate', what makes you unique, and what you want them to do for you.

Believe in yourself. A little positivity goes a long way.

With recruitment agencies, visibility is key. Avoid random attacks. They'll forget you as soon as you walk out the door.

Select three established agencies and develop a close working relationship.

Make reasonable demands on them. Don't be afraid to seek advice or an explanation as to why they don't call you.

Pursue the agents with the reputation rather than agencies. It's the people who matter most.

---

the other. Visibility and recognition is key, so the better you're known, the easier it is to get agencies to 'sell you', rather than just 'hold your CV on file'.

2. MAKE REASONABLE DEMANDS

If they have not recommended any jobs of late, call them up and politely ask why this is the case. If you think you should have been put forward for a role they have overlooked to tell you about, let them know. If they have advice to give, listen to it intently. Don't *always* take it, though: follow your own agenda.

Unfortunately, many agencies require you continually to apply for jobs that are advertised on their website. This could mean that they may not feel sufficiently enthusiastic about you or your CV to make the effort to contact you about a particular position before they post the ad. Keep talking to them, so that you can both better understand each other. And remember, you're not bothering them, you're keeping *you* top of *their* mind.

3. PURSUE THOSE AGENTS WHO HAVE A REPUTATION FOR GETTING RESULTS

I said 'agent', not 'agency'. If you connect with a particular agent or someone your friends have recommended, follow that person – wherever they go.

There are numerous excellent agencies out there, but I found these three to be particularly useful not only in getting me in the door but in providing good advice and ongoing support:

CPL   *cpl.ie*

Manpower   *manpower.ie*

HRM   *hrm.ie*

The Internet Search: How to Control the Beast

The internet is undoubtedly a powerful search-and-find tool: 70 percent of the job interviews I secured came directly from opportunities I spotted online. However, looking for a job on the internet can be an overwhelming and fruitless exercise. For example, when I first began my job search, I manically set up my details on any and every site I could think of – at home and abroad. Some interesting job alerts came my way:

1. *Ecumenical evangelist* Who knows?

2. *Blind dog trainer* My training experience, while significant, did not extend to real animals.

3. *Editor – of eighteenth-century historical publications* So there was a Henry the something and a Louis the something, and they were both sex-mad, war-mongering renegades. Yeah, I could do that. Where do I apply?

4. *Career-guidance counsellor* I know!

5. *Immigration supervisor* Don't ask me, I think it was something to do with my 'international' experience.

All amusing, but got me nowhere.

There are some simple ways, therefore, to cut down on wasted internet searching:

A. *Limit your search to the key sites only.* Within your specific field, there will be online recruitment sites which are updated daily. Find out which two or three are best in your industry, and register your core interests with them.

B. *Be discerning about your skills and experiences.* Tick key experiences only in the search boxes, and be specific about the industries you are looking to work in. No wishful thinking!

C. *Twice or three times a week only, do an early-morning scan of all chosen sites* as you finish off your breakfast coffee.

In my experience, the best sites in terms of job opportunities and good advice were:

1. *irishjobs.ie*

2. *recruitireland.ie*

3. The recruitment agency websites I mentioned earlier

Know Your Competition and What Advantages You Have Over Them

Ignoring the fact that numerous people, a mix of 'broad-strokers' and 'streamliners', are also competing for the job will hamper you. Compete! What do you have over someone with, say, a 'streamlined' CV? What do you know that they might not? There is no one like you out there, and that's a great strength, so play on it. Never downplay what makes you unique.

Look for 'In Between' Opportunities

Don't eliminate an opportunity just because it hasn't got the right pay packet or doesn't come with the same status as your previous roles. 'In between' roles tend not to have either of these, because they tend not to be permanent. But a reasonable salary for a reasonable challenge is better than no salary and no challenge at all, so approach every opportunity positively and with an open mind. This is a regret of mine. I was too picky too early and, although I eventually found well-paid roles, I should have supplemented the 'gap months' with some in-between opportunities.

So learn to say a big 'yes' much more often than you say 'no'. It is easier to get a job when you have a job, so grab work opportunities as they arise.

'In between' roles can be unpaid work experience in a new field, contract or part-time work, administrative jobs, the same role you did previously but for less money, a lesser role for less money, a different role with less money, and so on. In some ways it doesn't matter, as long as it's getting you out of the house and keeping you busy.

The average time spent on in-between roles tends to be six months: in other words, about as long as it takes for you to find the right role! So start saying 'yes' to in-between opportunities, but be very careful that this does not interfere with your goal of finding the right role. Never stop the search.

Top Tips for Getting Back in the Game

Create an up-to-date CV.

'Work' that contacts network, however small it may be. Remember to have the following prepared before you call: what are you good at, what are you willing to work at (from 'dream' to 'desperate'), what do you want them to do for you?

Be positive about your achievements. Believe in yourself or no one else will.

Go easy on the exuberance. Insincerity is easily spotted.

Make friends with the recruitment agents so that they 'sell you' rather than keep your details on file.

Follow agents with a good reputation. The recruitment business is all about people and connections.

Scale back your internet search to a few key sites only and be discerning about which boxes you tick when it comes to your work experience. Otherwise you'll be bombarded by reams of rubbish.

Know the competition and what you may have over them. Play on your uniqueness and personal attributes.

Consider 'in between' opportunities. Sometimes you need to take a quick step back to make a great leap forwards.

Never stop the search for the dream job, regardless of your circumstances.

6

CV Dilemmas and How to Fix Them

As we discussed previously, 'broad-strokers' have more difficulty opening doors than 'streamliners'. With streamliners, it is essentially a case of 'more of the same'. When you are a broad-stroker, you will have a mixed bag of experiences and responsibilities, so it takes a little work to understand what your next step should be. However, being a broad-stroker does give you flexibility too, so it's not all bad. Below are some tips for a broad-stroker on communicating the best of their collective experience.

1. FOCUS ON THE COMMON THREADS

When you look clearly at your varied experience, you will find elements that tie everything together – common strengths or responsibilities. No matter how varied your experiences have been, there are always common factors which define your working life. These should be summarised and presented at the beginning of your CV.

In the table below are examples of responsibilities and strengths which can be applied to a variety of situations.

Responsibilities	Strengths
New-opportunity creation	Drive, vision and initiative, courage, selling, relationship-building
Customer-relationship management:	Trust, communication, responsiveness, interpersonal and problem-solving abilities
Managing people	Leadership, team-building, motivation, communication, strategic ability
Managing varied projects	Flexibility, organisational agility and initiative, organising skills
Budget management	Honesty, reliability, an eye for detail
Creative decisions	Flair, ability to think outside the box
Administration	Being responsible, ability to take instructions and deliver to deadlines
Decision-making	Intelligence, leadership, independence, being responsible
Security	Being responsible, reliable, honest
Teamwork	People-sensitivity, ability to work within other people's agendas
Managing change	Flexibility, positivity, responsiveness

2. USE THE BEST EXPERIENCES THAT MATTER TO THE JOB YOU ARE APPLYING FOR

including temporary and voluntary positions.

3. THINK 'ACTIONS AND ACHIEVEMENTS', NOT 'EXPLANATION OR NARRATIVE'

Bear in mind that prospective employers will speed-read your CV and look out for key words only.

Creating a High-impact CV Structure

1. LEAD YOUR CV WITH A THREE-STATEMENT SUMMARY

Point to your overall experience and strengths, and your contribution to the organisation, in terms of the benefits you brought to it.

Collective Strengths and Achievements:
'I am an *experienced* manager/executive/professional with a *strong track record of achievement* across a number of business/technical/operational/financial areas, such as (examples could be: 'successfully managing projects', 'maintaining and exceeding the already high standards within the company', 'ensuring that the people around me were supported and equipped to deliver to tight targets' or 'maintaining accurate reports and daily records').

Your Contribution:
'I brought excellent organisational/technical/organisational/financial/communication/creative/leadership/administration skills in meeting the challenges faced.'

Which Delivered the Following Benefits to the Company:

Revenue increase

Cost reduction

Business improvement/productivity

Social/environmental impact

Customer experience/business reputation

Innovation

Execution/implementation

Financial responsibility

2. TELL THE STORY OF YOUR EXPERIENCE SO THAT YOU CLEARLY DICTATE THE CONCLUSION

You want the person reading your CV to think: this person has the right mix of skills and experience for *this* role. I want to meet him/her. *Don't expect the reader of your CV to do this themselves.* You should present the detail in a way that clearly leads the reader exactly where they need to go, i.e. to call you, not others, for an interview.

3. MAINTAIN *ONLY* TWO DIFFERENT VERSIONS OF YOUR CV

I am not a fan of having any more than two versions of a CV. I remember that at one point I had six different versions of my CV, all written from scratch for completely different roles. I was left feeling like a bit of a fraud, with no authentic sense of identity or career direction, and I'm sure this came across at the interview.

The two versions of your CV should incorporate the following:

VERSION 1: THE SUMMARY

Two pages only. This is used as an introduction only to contacts and agencies. It should consist of a two- to three-line achievement summary for each key role you have undertaken over the past five-plus years.

All content should be carefully chosen to be strictly about *achievements and results* (specifically quantifiable ones, such as percentage sales, revenue, number of customers managed/supported, number of products launched, and so on), *relevant competencies only*, and a *short summary of the role. Note: Do not include activities or job specifications.*

VERSION 2: THE ARCHIVE

Up to five pages. This outlines, in as much detail as possible:

> key achievements (professional, academic and personal)

> personal and professional strengths displayed

> key responsibilities

> relevant activities which helped you to achieve the above

The archive acts as the one and only document to be used to tailor a response around a job specification.

BENEFITS OF USING THE ARCHIVE APPROACH

A. It helps you maintain a stronger sense of your experience and what it says about your strengths. We can lose ourselves in the world of 'tailored CVs'.

B.   A stronger sense of direction as to what roles and responsibilities you are best suited to.

C.   It gives you more time, as you do not have to be continually rewriting your CV.

D.   There is less temptation to 'invent' – a truly dangerous thing. Lies will always surface!

Therefore, if the knowledge, skills or experience required for an advertised role are not reflected in your archive, the best thing is to pass on the opportunity.

Finally, we can sometimes forget that we have experience and skills if we haven't used them in a while, so don't be afraid to update your archive.

7

Make Your Money Work

Even if You Don't

EMPTY POCKETS NEVER HELD ANYONE BACK.
ONLY EMPTY HEADS AND EMPTY HEARTS CAN DO THAT
NORMAN VINCENT PEALE

Having little or no money can be a serious debilitator in life. It can cause untold strain in our lives. But think about it for a second. So can having no friends. Poor health. Family tragedy. A bad reputation. Living without self-respect or dignity. Ignorance. Lies. Guilt. Secrets. Loneliness. Feeling trapped. All of these things can drive financially secure people over the edge. So it's important to put things into perspective: money problems are not the only thing in life that cause strain. I know people who have accepted temporary poverty rather than enduring a bullying boss or a horrible spouse, and they don't regret a second of it.

We're talking about money here, because if we were all given a multi-million-euro severance package, redundancy and unemployment would be something to aspire to. We fear redundancy for lots of reasons, but mainly it is to do with our livelihood: how we will survive when the pay cheques stop coming. Essentially, money is very tied up with our perception of ourselves and others.

Having little or no money is only made worse by the stupid, desperate things we do to protect ourselves from financial insecurity. From borrowing excessive amounts, to drug dealing, extortion, lies, prostitution, theft and fraud, the world is full of stories of desperate and vulnerable people who will seemingly try anything to keep the wolf from the door.

Yes, it's a tough world. No question. And poverty makes it tougher. But being cash-poor, especially if it is temporary (i.e. for six months or so), is not the end of the world. Here are my tips on how you can survive it with your dignity and confidence intact.

1. GET AN HONEST ASSESSMENT AS TO HOW LONG YOU MAY BE OUT OF WORK

From recruitment agencies, your colleagues, or others. Then double it! That's probably how long you really will be unemployed, unless you're one of the lucky few.

2. GET AN HONEST ASSESSMENT AS TO HOW MUCH MONEY YOU WILL REALLY NEED FROM SOMEONE WHO KNOWS YOU AND YOUR LIFESTYLE

Listen to them carefully. Left to our own devices, we tend to go into furious denial about how much we really spend in a week. If you've never done this before, you will be amazed at the amount of money you waste on absolute rubbish.

3. COUNT OUT EVERY SINGLE CENT YOU CAN GET YOUR HANDS ON WITHIN A FEW WEEKS

We're talking redundancy packages, unemployment benefit, tax rebates, savings accounts, deposit accounts, prize bonds (your mother is probably 'minding' them for you). Don't forget paintings, crafts, old clothes and homeware which you can sell locally or on eBay.

4. CREATE A SPREADSHEET OF YOUR CURRENT CASH STATUS

and update it every day with the latest inflow/outflow. This prevents you from going into denial about where your money is going and, importantly, what you have left to spend. A handwritten sheet is better, because you can bring it everywhere with you.

5. TEMPORARILY CALL A HALT TO ANY UNNECESSARY SPENDING

We have unnecessary spending in many areas of our lives. Just because something is an important expenditure, it doesn't mean it is necessary at this point in your life. This may mean being more discerning in your weekly food shopping, or investment in expensive hobbies (cars, for example). For some, this may also involve calling your bank manager to organise a 'mortgage break'. While important, it may not be necessary, right at this point in time, to have a mortgage payment hanging over you. Many people take this option and it will relieve your financial pressure considerably while you arrange a solution to your work situation.

For some, socialising and retail therapy are the big expenses and if you really feel you need to blow off some steam, then make sure it is kept to once a month at the absolute most, and using money that you have *earned*, not borrowed. This is easier than you think. We don't need 'things' nearly as much as we think we do, and you will not miss them as much as you think you will. The novelty of a new pair of boots or a new mobile device, or the fun of an expensive night out, wears off very fast. So too does the craving to do it. Try it for yourself. Go without spending anything other than essentials for a week, and see how you feel. Sure, initially you will feel deprived, like you've missed out on something. But like all non-essentials, especially novelties, the need to show it off soon wears thin. You may find that it didn't suit you nearly as much as you'd hoped, and before you know it, the craving for something else kicks in.

In addition to not spending, with a little creativity, your current possessions may contain long-lost wonders. Very soon, you won't feel deprived about walking away,

---

TOP TIPS ON GETTING YOUR FINANCES IN ORDER

GET HONEST!

about how long you think you may be out of work. Then double it.

about how much money you will really need in total to make it through that time.

COUNT THE CASH

Where is all your money right now?

How long will it take to turn it into hard cash?

Document your spending. It won't seem real otherwise.

Create a spreadsheet on all daily outgoings and ingoings.

Compare it constantly to actual cash you have available. You will then see when the money is due to run out.

Temporarily cut back on all unnecessary spending. Ask yourself over and over: 'Do I really need to buy this right now?' If the answer is not a resolute 'yes' (food, rent, utility bills, school books, and so on), don't buy it now. Maybe next week!

---

but strong and self-sufficient, not to mention happy that you no longer need so many of the irrelevant things in life, and are no longer the 'advertiser's fool'.

You see, there is a big difference between not spending and not having. And in contrast, there is a big difference between having and spending. And I'm not just talking about self-esteem – the key reason for spending in the first place. I'm talking about the practicalities of having lots of fun times without ever putting your hand in your pocket.

Things to Do When Cash Is Tight

1. PICK UP THE LOCAL EVENT GUIDE

at your newsagents or supermarket. You'll be amazed at the number of musical, art and drama events which are free of charge – from lunchtime dramas, early-evening jazz sessions, book launches, product launches, art exhibitions, fashion shows, dance shows, classes, children's shows. There are endless ways to spend enjoyable hours with your kids and friends without spending more than the price of a drink or a coffee.

You may find that some events are invitation-only, but hey, arrive dressed up with a smile, and chances are good you'll gain access.

2. LEARN THE ART OF BROWSING

Don't be even remotely intimidated by snotty sales assistants in designer stores. You are entitled to try out stuff with no pressure to buy. So go ahead. Pick two or three of their most amazing items, try them on, and daydream. Then, when you're bored, place them neatly back in their place, thank the assistants, and leave.

For men, there's the sport car and motorbikes to test-drive. Act like you know it all, re-invent yourself for an hour as a successful anyone, and get yourself a free buzz for the afternoon.

3. TAKE ADVANTAGE OF FREE OR DISCOUNTED PRODUCTS OR SERVICES

such as free career assessments, or donating yourself as a model for student hairdressers, massage therapists or make-up artists. There are a number of great sites, like *jumbletown.ie/forums/index.php* or *ebay.ie* and *free-stuff.co.uk,* where you can get everything and anything free of charge or, at the very least, at a discount. Check them out: you'll never look back.

4. TRADE IN YOUR OLD CLOTHES, SHOES AND OTHER ITEMS

for 'new' at second-hand stores or with your friends. Make a night of it. In a recent fashion interview, Victoria Beckham was quoted as saying: 'It's amazing what people throw out.' So if she thinks that, well Lordy, it must be true! So go for a rummage in your friends' wardrobes and start negotiating.

5. LET PEOPLE KNOW YOU ARE TRYING HARD TO CUT BACK

on your spending until you find a job. Let them treat you instead. Most people are happy to stand a good friend a lunch or dinner in these kind of circumstances.

6. SOCIALISE AT HOME

A great pasta dish served with sparkling wine costs no more than €15 for four people. Many of the most enjoyable meals I have ever had were long rainy nights spent indoors, with pasta and beer, wrapped up warm in the company of my favourite people.

7. Give Yourself a Weekly Budget and Try to Stick to It

Believe me, the sense of achievement and pride you get when you come in on, or under, budget is immense.

8. Pay in Cash

Credit cards are one of the biggest reasons why people find themselves in debt – and expensive debt at that. Cut them up. Hide them. Don't bring them out with you. Trust me, you'll soon get used to it, and you'll realise that you didn't need either them or the junk you buy with them nearly as much as you had thought. Cash is your only friend during financial downtimes.

9. Stop Wasting Money

We all do it, even when we don't have it to waste. Check out the book *Stop Wasting Your Money* by Conor Pope for hundreds of useful tips, from avoiding packaged foods to doing regular checks to ensure that your debt and insurance providers are providing the best possible deal for you. Very often, they aren't!

The important thing here is that we often spend inordinate amounts of time trying to scrimp and save on the small things but ignore the big expenses, like debt and insurance. A few calls that will take five minutes each could save you hundreds, if not thousands, or euro. It doesn't make sense not to try.

10. Ask for a Discount

This is another thing which makes many Irish people nervous, but there are easy ways to get started. First of all, fully avail of all vouchers or loyalty cards distributed by retail outlets, petrol stations, coffee shops and supermarkets. It all adds up nicely over the months – and comes in return for just thirty seconds of your time completing a simple form. If such loyalty schemes are not available, haggle: offer them a good price or ask for something free of charge. The manager is the best person to negotiate with.

TOP TIPS ON LIVING WELL ON A LIMITED BUDGET

Scan the event guides. You'll be amazed at the number of fantastic things going on in your town or city which are free of charge.

Learn the art of browsing. There are tons of top-end luxury products to play with for an afternoon.

Take advantage of freebies. Thay are all over the place: freebie websites, trials.

Trade in your old stuff for new. Or at least new to you. Whose style do you like? Go rummage, and offer something back.

Let people treat you.

Socialise at home. It's fun. It's cheaper. There's no closing time.

Give yourself a weekly budget and compete with yourself to stick to it.

Hide your credit card. Cash is your only friend during financial downtimes.

Stop wasting your money. We all do it. Look for the hidden costs in your life. Focus on the big things first, like debt and insurance costs. Make full use of loyalty cards and vouchers.

Join the credit union. Flexibility is an important financial tool.

This practice works best in electrical-goods outlets, DIY stores, restaurants, hotels and designer shops, but you can try it anywhere: confidently ask the manager for something off to secure a cash sale or to facilitate a purchase of a number of items. If he or she says no, tell them nicely that they should, but don't take it personally. Move on to the next place. But do ask. The worst thing they can do is say 'no'!

11. SET UP A CREDIT UNION ACCOUNT

If you have any loans, be they credit-card loans or car loans, set up a credit-union account as a priority. Credit unions are generally far more flexible than other financial institutions when it comes to paying off debt.

Making a Quick Buck

Aside from making your money go further, you can also add some cash to the picture in any number of ways:

1. ACCEPT PART-TIME OR SHORT-TERM WORK

Ideally, but not necessarily, this work should be related to the area you are interested in. Take anything that will get you back into a routine. It's true that it's easier to get a job if you have a job, so the important thing is to *say yes to the temporary offers*. You'll regret it if you don't; I certainly did. And don't worry about the impact on your CV: you don't have to include it or tell anyone about it. I know I sound like a 'pile it high, sell it cheap' recruitment agency here, but the saying that 'A reasonable salary is better than no salary at all' is true – something my pride would not let me accept. So swallow your pride and get working.

Here are a few ideas that worked for some when jobs in their field of expertise were not available:

A. *Teach* anything related to your chosen career at your local college or secondary school. I lectured in entrepreneurial studies and drew on the years I had spent working with these brilliant people. Otherwise, teach English to foreign-language students: place an advert in the newspaper or drop your CV into the local language schools.

B. *Temp* as a receptionist, painter/decorator, website designer, product tester, software programmer, chef, marketer, PC troubleshooter, gardener, clothes-maker – whatever comes your way. It doesn't have to be included in your CV unless you consider it to be relevant. And it shouldn't interfere with your job search as long as you keep your mobile phone close to hand.

C. *Mind children* for friends, family and neighbours. (Unless you have a tendency to turn into a neurotic chain-smoker at the sight of a screaming child; in that case, maybe you should stick to pulling pints.)

2. Sell Your Unwanted Items

On *ebay.ie* or *greenmetropolis.co.uk* (for books), or organise a car-boot sale or a stand at a local fête. When you take the time to do a really thorough spring-clean, you will be amazed at the stuff you have but never use, such as homeware, furniture, keyboards, cordless phones, clothes, cameras, kitchen appliances, bedding, toys, gardening tools – all of which could make you a few quid. So scrub them up and get them out there. The couple of hours it may take to do this could yield you hundreds of euro.

One of my friends created six baskets of age-relevant toys, put up signs in crèches and supermarkets, and earned back a quarter of their original price. Better than a slap in the chops!

Another couple I know got together with four of their neighbours and had a huge garden sale. They promoted locally, spoke on local radio, and blogged. They sold kitchen equipment, blankets, jewellery, glasses and lamps, and even picked up some bargains themselves.

3. Get Paid for Your Hobby

If you love gardening, website development, PCs, cooking, painting or dancing, offer your services for a small fee. Put a notice in local newspapers and colleges, and on company noticeboards and blog sites.

4. Sign Up with Market-research Agencies to Participate in Focus Groups

These agencies are always looking for people. You can earn €50 to €75 a slot. Check their contact details in the Golden Pages. In addition, you can sign on for online surveys and get paid. Check out *free-stuff.co.uk* and *irish-opinions.com*.

5. Sign Up for Unemployment Benefit

This is another thing I avoided for months because I couldn't get beyond the feeling that if you're 'scratching', then you must have reached rock bottom. And I wasn't ready to accept that I had sunk that low. For me, the dole queue was a place for losers and scroungers. Also, I was a little in denial, as I thought I would find a job the very next day and, as a result, it wouldn't be worth the effort. Right? Nope!

When I eventually signed on after the third month, the assessing officer confirmed that I was not alone in this, and that he sees more and more professionals waiting for months before signing on, with the same attitude about reaching 'rock bottom'. His take on things?: 'You've worked hard for years and paid your taxes. This money is yours, and signing on is only temporary.' Thankfully, I only had to sign on once a month, and only three times in all. And yes, I dreaded shuffling in line with all the other hard-luck cases. (The extra-large beany hat with detachable dreadlocks and oversized sunglasses helped!). The additional €750 per month helped me hold on to more of my redundancy package than I would have been able to otherwise.

6. REVIEW YOUR TAX SITUATION

If you've worked consistently, paid tax and been unemployed for a few months, you may be entitled to a tax rebate, using a P50 form. Get advice on this. Call your local Revenue office or search online. In addition, you may be surprised about what expenses (bin charges, medical fees) you can claim back. The Revenue will *not* contact *you*; you are responsible for the management of your own taxes, so be proactive and go online to *revenue.ie* or call them for guidance. They are very helpful and it doesn't take long to find out what you're entitled to.

7. SET YOURSELF UP AS A BUSINESS

If either you or your partner is doing contract work, consider setting yourself up as a business. It may make a significant difference to your working capital and cash flow. Expenses such as petrol, a mobile phone, rent and utilities can all be either partly or fully written off against your earnings, thereby significantly reducing your tax bill. The only downside is the tax return – which, by the way, only takes an hour or two to complete online. Do give this some serious consideration. Check out *revenue.ie* or *startingabusinessinireland.com* for some valuable tips.

8. Apply for Rebates

Have you applied for every type of rebate you are entitled to, such as mortgage interest relief at source? Not sure? Then check it out. No one is going to knock on your door to give you money; you have to chase it. Make that call to the helpful folk at the Revenue or your financial advisor!

9. Set Up a Blog

Check out *BlogCash-Guide.com* for ideas on how you can make money from doing this.

10. Make Your Redundancy Package Work

Some people do amazing things with even small amounts. They purchase properties, set up businesses, change career, invest in pensions – and improve their lives considerably. Others, by contrast, blow a €50,000 windfall on God knows what, and are still living at home at thirty. Plenty of people are blissfully oblivious to the need to make their finances secure and assume that someone, somewhere, will save them if problems arise.

There is definitely a trick to financial management and making your cash go further. A lot of it is instilled in us from an early age. So if you are one of the lucky ones who receives a windfall in the form of a redundancy package, it is worthy getting proper financial advice on what to do with it. Don't just stick it your bank account and get complacent, thinking that your financial problems are over: it will be all gone before you know it. In the months before and after my wedding, I found myself out of work, and the windfall I received saved me during this downtime. Yes, I had other plans for the money – I had wanted to buy a house, go back to college etc, but thus had to wait longer to do this. In the end, I was immensely grateful for the safety net.

Below are some tips on managing any package you receive:

1. PAY OFF YOUR DEBTS

Every single one of them. Even paying a chunk off your mortgage will help ease your repayment burden and increase your financial worth. It's a bore but a valuable thing to do.

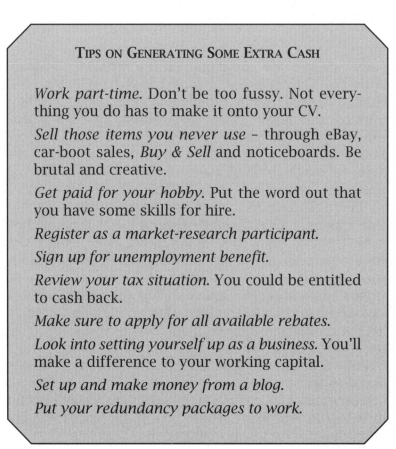

TIPS ON GENERATING SOME EXTRA CASH

Work part-time. Don't be too fussy. Not everything you do has to make it onto your CV.

Sell those items you never use – through eBay, car-boot sales, *Buy & Sell* and noticeboards. Be brutal and creative.

Get paid for your hobby. Put the word out that you have some skills for hire.

Register as a market-research participant.

Sign up for unemployment benefit.

Review your tax situation. You could be entitled to cash back.

Make sure to apply for all available rebates.

Look into setting yourself up as a business. You'll make a difference to your working capital.

Set up and make money from a blog.

Put your redundancy packages to work.

2. WORK IT AROUND YOUR CURRENT WORK SITUATION

Is it part-time or contract? Then you may have no choice but keep at least some of it in a high interest deposit account for easy access. If you have dependents, then keeping it close to you may be the only choice you have.

3. KEEP YOUR PENSION GOING

Pensions are getting bad press these days, and for the wrong reason. People are now turned off them because of the much publicised dramatic loss in value and the horror stories about those who plan to retire soon. The problem isn't the pension itself, but the way in which the money was invested – and it appears now that bad investment decisions were made along the way. The truth is though, I have never found an advisor who does *not* think that pensions are the most tax-efficient way of saving your money in the long term. The big question is, and one which you now have increasing control over, is about how your pension fund should be invested. If you have a conservative outlook on money, then voice these requirements to your pension fund managers. Don't allow them to take unnecessary risks with your money. If they don't listen, look for another manager. The important point here is to keep your pension going and if you haven't already, get started. The adverts on TV are correct. You will regret if you don't. Make a quick call to an independent broker or search online. Ignorance is not an option with regard to securing your financial future.

4. INVEST YOUR MONEY

If you have managed to find permanent work, invest some of the money, even if it's only €5,000. Go online, read the financial pages of the newspaper, or ask people in the know whether now is a good time to invest in the stock market, bonds, property, deposit accounts, and so on. But don't take risks on something you know nothing about. If you are not willing to do some research, you're probably better off putting the money into a deposit account.

Things You Should Never Do When You're Time-rich and Cash-poor

1. GAMBLE

I'm talking about online poker, the stock market, over-subscribing to the Lotto, backing horses and getting involved in 'quick-win' pyramid schemes. And if you absolutely *must* gamble, then *only* do it in an area where you've proven yourself to be adept when you had the cash. You may as well throw your money down the drain otherwise. Common sense dictates, though, that if you haven't already been successful at any of the above, particularly when you had spare cash, you will not be any luckier when you're strapped. Don't fool yourself; walk away.

2. BORROW

Unless it's a small, manageable amount, don't borrow money unless you have a realistic and fully worked-out plan as to *how* and *when* you are going to pay it off. Just don't do it otherwise! Take on a second job pulling pints or cleaning windows if you're really that stuck! And if you really need to borrow, steer clear of the banks and opt for a credit union account or approach a *wealthy* relative (not a poor one). They are considerably more flexible and forgiving.

3. BE A PHARMACEUTICAL GUINEA PIG

You've surely heard enough scare stories to know that this is a big no-no.

8

Lose Your Job — Keep Your Sanity!

YOU ARE INDEBTED TO YOUR IMAGINATION FOR
THREE-FOURTHS OF YOUR IMPORTANCE –
DAVID GARRICK

Dealing with Long-term Unemployment

For me, 'long-term' is four to six months or more. Maybe
I'm impatient and have an exaggerated sense of my life
flying by. For others, it is somewhere beyond twelve
months. For those who have been unemployed for longer
than this, being out of the workforce for such an extended period of time can weigh you down like a boulder
on your head. If affects how you see everything around
you and how you think others see you. This is where serious mental discipline is required. Don't become your
own worst enemy by thinking the worst of yourself and
hence of everyone else around you.

SAD FACT: Most people are in a rut because they
choose to be.

SADDER FACT: People think there is nothing valuable for them to do because they choose to think that.

SADDEST FACT: We are what we do, and we do what we think.

As someone who experienced being out of work for a longer-than-expected period, I know how difficult it is to feel like a valued fee-paying member of society when no one has returned your calls in endless weeks, the agencies keep 'losing' your CV, and even the neighbour's dog bumps right into you because he was too busy looking at an empty crisp bag on the street. (This actually happened to me!) Yes, it is really cold on the outside, and you can start to identify with Michael Douglas's character in the movie *Falling Down*. But here's the reality check: you feel like that because you choose to. That was said to me by my long-suffering husband after he came home to find me moping around the house in my pyjamas. He'd had enough, and told me so.

The important thing to remember is that quite a lot of working people feel the same way every day: they get passed over for promotion, get dumped, make bad choices, and so on. The circumstances are different, but the feeling is the same: the world's a bitch, and everyone's conspiring to keep me down.

The good news is that with a little effort, creativity and mental discipline, you can enhance your value and sense of worth, whether you are working or not.

How to See Yourself in the Best Light

The exercise below might sound unnecessary for those who consider themselves too down-to-earth to be bothered to do it, but you'll be amazed by how much better you feel when you do it. I and my fellow 'redundees' sniggered childishly though this at a post-redundancy workshop, but I was amazed by how many times I rummaged around looking for it later on.

1. Write down the top five most important things you have achieved in both your personal and professional life. Things you are really, truly, honestly proud of. Don't think it, write it. It appears more real when it's down on paper. If you can't think of five, three will do.

2. Then write, beside each one, the key strengths it took to achieve it. People skills? Competent decision-making? A good eye for opportunity? Leadership? Good insight, financial prudence, political savvy, kindness, compassion, courage, empathy, passion, resilience, creativity, sense of ownership and responsibility, powers of persuasion, dedication, clear-thinking, patience, dignity, strong values, independence, determination?

3. Then write down the top five to ten best things that have been said either about you or to you. Real things. Truths. Can't think of any? I know. it's difficult to remember them. I'm not sure why, but it seems far easier to remember the bad things people say about you than the good things. See below for some examples to get you thinking:

'I know you'll be a great success.''You're the best manager I've ever had.' 'You're smarter than most!' 'The customers love you.' 'You make us feel special.' 'You're a brilliant friend. Always there when I need you.' 'You're a safe pair of hands.' 'You always know what to do.' 'You give really good advice.''You treat everyone fairly.' 'I really love working with you.' 'You're such good fun.' 'I know I can always rely on you.' 'You're the most positive person I know.' 'You inspired me to change my job/life.' 'I trust your judgement more than I trust most others.' 'You make me laugh.' 'You challenge me and made me sit up and think.' 'You are always so welcoming and hospitable.' 'You're one of the most able people in the team.' 'I always know I can rely on you.'

4   Keep this in a safe place, and at some point every day, read it carefully. Every day.

Remember, you are no different from anyone who has a job. They are neither better nor worse than you. They too have to put their best foot forward and stay positive. They too can feel trapped, disillusioned and unsupported – just like you. They have bad days where they wish they could be anywhere else. The only difference is their circumstances . . . and, of course, their bank balance. But in front of an interviewer, it's irrelevant.

How to Work When You're Not Working

NOBODY CAN THINK STRAIGHT WHO DOES NOT WORK.
IDLENESS WARPS THE MIND.
HENRY FORD

When you are unemployed, the easiest thing in the world to do is mope around and think about how unlucky you are and how lucky everyone else is, how unfair the world is . . . blah, blah, blah. True as all of this may be, thinking it as you sit on your proverbial big pile of worms does not solve your problem. Not even close. So stop beating yourself up because you have too much time on your hands. Your priority now is making your time matter, and there are countless ways to do this. Here are some of the things that worked for me:

1. WORK FOR NOTHING

How many people do you know have small businesses and would sincerely appreciate a few days of your time to help with things like planning, administration, tele-sales, packing and posting, and cleaning – all for the price of your lunch. Plenty, I would say, so offer your services for a few days here and there, particularly to people who work in your area of interest. The routine and sense of well-being it gives will far outweigh the loss of income. If the days are becoming regular, then by all means work out a fair renumeration.

2. UP-SKILL

There are any number of correspondence and online courses as well as evening and weekend workshops you can attend without it interfering with your job search. Don't think you don't have the time to do this, because you absolutely do. The best way to achieve this is by setting aside the same time slot every day (preferably in the late morning) to up-skilling. Put yourself on a course at this time and, as the days and weeks go by, you will be pleasantly surprised by what you have learned. Examples of courses I did both online or free at the local enterprise centre are:

Setting up your own business It was a nice idea, but I decided it was too lonely a project.

Website development Forgotten everything!

Creative writing And here I am!

Dress-making I had a far-fetched notion that I would make my wedding dress but took my tutor's uproarious laughter as a bad sign.

Microsoft Office applications I 'mastered' Excel.

Financial management for small businesses

Car maintenance But I would still prefer to eat my own toenails than change a tyre.

There are hundreds of courses available, and if you have even an hour each day, it would be a real waste if you didn't take advantage. So make a decision to do it, sign up, and follow through.

3. JOIN A POLITICAL PARTY

Well, you don't have to join, but gatecrash their get-to-gethers. They are all so desperate to get your vote, they will welcome you with open arms. But not only will you meet some very interesting people and potential job contacts, it's also a great place to discuss your own issues – not to mention the free tea and cake. I attended a Green Party get-together one evening with a friend and had such a laugh I almost became a paid-up member. My brush with the Progressive Democrats (RIP) left me with a stronger opinion of their compassionate side towards the vunerable in society (i.e. the unemployed: I was a single-issue gatecrasher) than I had previously given them credit for.

4. VOLUNTEER

I know we all put this down on our New Year's Eve resolution list with not even the slightest intention of doing anything about it. But if you have additional time in the morning or afternoon, make the decision to commit, and you will be delighted that you did. Most local charities, hospitals and day-care centres are crying out for local support from reliable, honest people. You will be inspired and humbled by the challenges faced by those less advantaged than you, and inspired again by your own contribution. And if you don't fancy hospitals or charities, why not volunteer at the local arts centre or community sports centre. Again, like up-skilling, just make a decision that you are going to do it, make some calls and set aside a particular time of the week to participate. It's not hard. I volunteered for a local arts centre, and watching sixteen-year-olds on stage in a packed auditorium made me realise that there were harder things out there than looking for a job.

5. GO PUBLIC ABOUT WHAT'S BOTHERING YOU

Begin blogging on the issues you are facing (great fun, and instant, with very broad reach). Check out *Bloggers-Guide.com* or just contribute to existing sites. Alternatively, write stern letters to newspapers: you might even get published as a star letter and win a bottle of whiskey – no, I never actually won a bottle of whiskey but some people do. I have had letters published on waiting ninety minutes in the rain for a train (during which time I was blessed with the epiphany that I needed to move back to Dublin), poor press coverage of a canoeing event in which my husband participated, and a rare positive experience with clampers. It's a bit of fun!

6. GET BACK IN TOUCH WITH OLD FRIENDS

Use available time to catch up with old friends. Our busy lives have had a negative effect on our ability to keep in touch with some great people we have met. Now that you have the time, track them down. Sign on to *facebook.com*. It only takes a few minutes. And aside from cyber-stalking (which I don't do!), there is nothing better than getting a funny, uplifting email from a great person from your past.

7. TRAVEL

If you can't afford to travel abroad, travel around your own country. It never ceases to amaze me how little we explore our own country – or even our own county. So get out and act like a tourist for the day. I wandered the length and breadth of Kildare and bored everyone with my 'stunning' (!) photos of the Bog of Allen and a famine graveyard! Well, at least *I* had fun.

8. CLEAN UP YOUR HOUSE

Clutter, grime and stuffiness can sap your energy and motivation, so make sure you take the time to clear away the dishes, put everything back into its place, clean the surfaces and open the windows. And no, it won't take you all day: you don't live in a castle!

9. FOLLOW YOUR DREAMS

You have time on your hands, so why not have a go at something you have always wanted to try but could not find the time to do. Now you have it (stop saying you don't, you do!). If you dreamed of being an actor, writer, sportswriter, entrepreneur, inventor or whatever, you don't have to spend money to get in there. Sign up for drama, design, business-start-up or writing classes and re-invent yourself. Review a local event (or a national one, if you're feeling brave) and send in weekly reports to a few publications. Don't look for a fee: this isn't why you're doing it. But you never know, someone, sometime, may need to fill in a gap; they may appreciate your persistence and slot you in. How do you know if you don't try? You have nothing to lose. So have a think about what you would do if you didn't have to work for your pay cheque. In the words of Goethe: 'Whatever you dream you can do, begin it. Boldness has genius, power and magic in it. Begin it now.'

I pursued my dreams of writing a novel (it was awful but I loved doing it), and this self-help guide. My friend pursued her dream of setting up a website for the local sourcing of environmentally friendly and organic products and materials. She's still trying – and loving – it. Another trained as a landscaper/gardener and never went back to full-time office-based employment. He's too busy! So there you go: when one door closes . . . Start small. Make it happen. You know you want to.

10. STOP RESISTING

This is not really in the 'work' category, but it's really important as a way of motivating you to change your life and get you working. I don't mean to sound like a psychologist, but what you resist, persists. Denial is the glue that holds our resistance in place and prevents us from moving on. Everyone denies, and it's not always a bad thing. In some cases, it is an important survival skill. But sometimes in denying what is happening around you, you are blocked from learning from the situation and resolving it. You will also invariably turn it on yourself or those closest to you. You see this everywhere. Denial can be really bad for you and can make you feel stuck.

The most important starting point is to find the words that honestly describe your current situation, and then, when that is done, to describe how you really, truly feel. Write them down if you have to. The next step is to ask yourself why you feel like that. Most people do not need the services of a trained counsellor to get to the heart of this. Sometimes, honest self-reflection, or a long chat with a trusted friend, will set you on a better road.

TOP TIPS ON WORKING WHEN NOT WORKING

Get into the right frame of mind. Complete the exercise on 'Seeing yourself in the best possible light' and pin it to your noticeboard.

Work for nothing. It's about routine and well-being.

Upskill. Career or leisure, get learning again.

Join a political party. Good contacts, free therapy, free tea.

Volunteer. You'll see there are harder things out there than looking for a job.

Go public about what's bothering you. Letters, blogs. The internet is your oyster. It's fun.

Turn into a tourist (Ditch the báinín!).

Clean your house. Dirt and clutter can zap your energy.

Follow your dreams. Begin it now. You have the time.

Stop resisting. What you resist, persists.

The point is that this brings not only acceptance of your situation and how you honestly feel about it, but motivation to move forward in a more positive, constructive way than you may have done previously.

Make the Most of Your 'Leisure' Time

Unemployment also colours your view of leisure time. The things we like to do in the evenings, like curl up with a book or lounge in front of the TV, lose their gloss when we're unemployed because, well, we can potentially do that all day anyway. But more importantly, you want your leisure time to *mean* something else. Here are a few things that worked for me and helped me much more than watching a *Friends* re-run.

1. GROW THINGS

There is something calming and inspiring about planting something, whether it's flowers, vegetables, shrubs or herbs, and watching it grow. It makes you feel part of something more important than you. I took to planting daffodil and tulip bulbs. Hundreds of them. And they still come up in droves every spring, as a big colourful reminder of their role in helping me through those long days.

2. BUILD THINGS

The time I spent on redecoration was one of my most enjoyable projects. Having spent so much time in the house, little things that had previously gone unnoticed were glaring and irritating. So I painted walls, cleared out rooms and hired a plasterer to move doors and build walls in order to make more use of the space. The effort – and €1,400 investment – paid off, as it added €20,000 to the value of the house. I also tried my hand at furniture-making with spare wood that had been sitting in the shed for five years. The bench and small table are still sitting in the garden, and still look great. I would never have taken on any of these things if I hadn't been forced to stay at home for months on end. I didn't know I had it in me.

3. GET ACTIVE

Do sports. Any type. If you haven't yet taken up a sport – do it. Do it today. Whether it's power-walking, soccer, dancing, running, swimming, sailing or golf, whatever it is, do it. Do it for one exuberant hour each day. It's a cliché, but you will feel immensely better afterwards. I hate sports, so I eventually forced myself to take a brisk fifty-minute round-trip walk into town to buy the paper every morning – in rain or sunshine. I was just happy that I managed to get my lazy ass out the door. It kept my head clear and kept me in a positive frame of mind (most of the time).

4. GET MARRIED TO THE MAN OR WOMAN OF YOUR DREAMS

OK, maybe that just applies to me!

TOP TIPS ON HOW TO USE LEISURE TIME TO HELP KEEP YOU MOTIVATED

Grow things (in your garden, not your cupboard). Trees, flowers, herbs. There is something calming about watching something you planted grow.

Build things. Paint, repair, reuse and renovate. The creative process will help you feel like you have something to show for your day.

Get active. It's not a myth that fitness helps your happiness and well-being. Get physical for at least an hour a day.

The Extra Dimensions Hobbies and Interests Give You

1. You're More Interesting

Hobbies and interests will feed your well-being and give you an extra dimension that a prospective employer will appreciate.

The point is that when you make a strong act of committing to projects, hobbies or sports which you enjoy and apply yourself to them loyally – for a minimum of one to two hours a day – you'll feel a hundred times better about everything else around you, even the horrible stuff like looking for a job.

2. You're More Focused on the Here and Now

The psychological and physical benefits of focusing your attention on physical activity such as exercise or a hobby has been well documented. It forces you to zone in on the moment and forget your worries, past or present – all of which clears your head and helps you handle your circumstances better.

3. You're More in Control

Committing a pre-defined time each day to hobbies or sport actually gives you back control – over your day and over your time. This is useful, particularly when you are not able to do this within the working world.

4. You're More Confident

Committing to other things beyond your job search dilutes your sense of pained desperation at interviews and networking meetings. Reason: you're not thinking as much about the job-seeking because other things have filled your day, and these things will fill your conversation too. This translates into a calmer, more centred you – which in turn releases pressure on everyone around you. And when that pressure is released, it is amazing the ideas you and other people come up with to help you.

How to Get Out There with Confidence

So you're browsing in a fabulous store, changing into another glamorous designer dress you could never hope to afford, when you hear a voice from the past, a voice you would rather not hear, chatting – loudly and amiably – with the snotty sales assistants who had earlier gone out of their way to ignore you! This exuberant chat can only mean one thing: the 'voice' is purchasing.

OK, maybe on this occasion it is acceptable to sit it out in the dressing room until closing time! But the reality is that you are going to bump into people you know all the time – including people you would rather not see, such as ex-colleagues, ex-bosses, ex-friends – so you need to be ready to deal with their questions and your potential discomfort, their good news and your possible jealousy, their social exuberance and, perhaps, your loneliness. And the bad news is that avoiding the situation is not the answer, easy though it is. These are your streets too, your shops, your parks, your pubs, your cafés, your theatres. You're entitled to be here. So go out there, hold your head high, and tread your territory.

Tips on getting out there with confidence

1. CHOOSE THE RIGHT PEOPLE

Meet people who wish the very best for you and are not affected by whether or not you're working. Avoid those who wish to keep you down. Cut them out of your life completely if you have to. This was a difficult thing for me to come to terms with, and I know that certain friendships suffered as a result of the time I spent unemployed. On the other hand, I made some fantastic new friends.

2. GO OUT AS OFTEN AS YOU CAN

Even if it's just for an hour: just one friendly face in the crowd is all you need. Be around strangers too. Be seen. You'll be happier that you did. And most importantly, you won't seem as though you have anything to hide. Because you don't.

3. MAKE AN EFFORT WITH YOUR APPEARANCE

'Shabby' equals 'down' in most people's minds. Groom. Wear nice clothes. Walk tall. Be seen to be looking well and in good spirits. Perception is reality for those who see you.

4. DON'T ACT SILLY

Remember the scene in *The Full Monty* when the main character and his son, while waiting at the father's ex-partner's workplace, start messing with a flex and nearly break it? You don't want people watching you doing something stupid, then uttering those dreaded words: 'Not surprised he's unemployed.' So keep your wits about you when you're out and about.

5. SEEM HAPPY TO SEE PEOPLE

Even if you're not. Approach them if you think you've been seen. Don't avoid anyone except the bitchy and the boastful.

6. BE READY FOR THEIR QUESTIONS

Such as 'What are you doing now?' The answer to this question obviously relates to work, but you can easily turn your answer round to include any interesting hobbies, child-rearing, training, part-time work or voluntary work you are doing. Talk happily about it. Make it matter. Because it does. People will also want to know who else you are in contact with. So let them know (and even mention those with whom you have occasional contact). It is important to give off the impression that your life is continuing happily along, that you have plenty of friends and that you are *not* at home feeling sorry for yourself. However, don't be afraid to add that you haven't yet found the right role: you never know what information people may have that could help you.

7. THROW A FEW COMPLIMENTS INTO THE CONVERSATION

Goodwill is something confident, happy people have in abundance. So get in there with a few kind words of your own. It will make you feel good too.

8. DON'T BAD-MOUTH ANYONE IF MEETING EX-COLLEAGUES

No matter how justified or how much anyone tempts you to do it. You will immediately appear bitter.

9. CONGRATULATE THE PERSON IF GOOD NEWS HAS RECENTLY COME THEIR WAY

But don't overdo it.

10. DON'T STAY TOO LONG

The longer you stay, the more you say, so make your excuses and leave early.

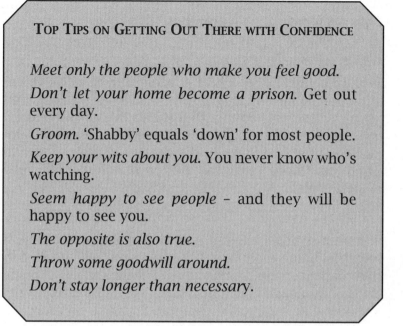

TOP TIPS ON GETTING OUT THERE WITH CONFIDENCE

Meet only the people who make you feel good.

Don't let your home become a prison. Get out every day.

Groom. 'Shabby' equals 'down' for most people.

Keep your wits about you. You never know who's watching.

Seem happy to see people – and they will be happy to see you.

The opposite is also true.

Throw some goodwill around.

Don't stay longer than necessary.

Handling Negative Thoughts

There's an old saying that goes: 'What you wish for others, you wish for yourself.' And I think there's some truth in it. What we bring into our lives is directly related to what is going on in our inner world.

When we are not where we want to be job- or career-wise, it is perfectly acceptable to feel a little envious of those who *appear* to be doing better than us. A little envy is healthy and helps to spur us on to do better. It becomes destructive, however, when it begins to pollute the mind with defeatism and bad feelings. When you're unemployed, feeling negative is the easiest thing in the world, but actually, this has less to do with the fact that you are unemployed than with the side effects of unemployment, including isolation and boredom.

Tips on Managing Negative Thinking

1. Don't Think Too Much

Human beings have a great capacity for negative thinking if left alone for long periods. So stop thinking and get busy. Fill your days with positive things and people: hobbies, socialising, job-hunting, volunteering and training. The more you have to do, the less time you have to dwell on things, and the better it will be for your mental health.

2. Keep the Amount of Time You Spend Alone to a Minimum

It is abundantly true that isolation makes you crazy. It certainly made me crazy. I talked to the television, carried on conversations even when the person was already off the phone, and became obsessively interested in the National Geographic TV channel. So make no more excuses. Get out, out, out! Have those drinks, coffees and lunches. And don't wait for people to call you: call people up and invite *them* out. Spend time with your friends, parents, siblings, aunts and uncles. In fact, with anyone who is even vaguely happy to see you and wishes you well. It only seems like an effort to drive forty minutes to see someone because you have so much emotional baggage to take along with you. Drop the baggage and drive.

3. Don't Obsess Over What Is Going on With Other People

In fact, give it little or no thought. Regardless of the perception you may have, nobody's life is perfect, and much of what we all do from day to day is routine, even mundane, regardless of our circumstances. We all have our good days and bad days. You should have enough to do with your time. And if somebody appears happy and fulfilled, it probably has as much to do with their natural mental state as their circumstances.

4. Avoid Bitchy or Boastful People

These types will bring you down faster than your circumstances, so make your excuses and make a resolution not to spend time with them.

5. Believe in Yourself

Tell yourself again and again that your time will come. Because it will. Read over your 'truth file', with your key achievements, strengths and personal endorsements, and take encouragement from it. Your time will come, so don't think about giving up.

6. Ask Successful People for Advice

Not even the most successful people in the world can claim that they did it all alone. They too have received and accepted good advice and support – and made plenty of mistakes. So swallow your pride, ask those who are getting the breaks what their secret is, and listen!

Tips on Managing Negativity

Think less; do more.

Get out of the house. Isolation makes you crazy.

Stop comparing. You have no idea what's really going on in other people's lives.

Believe that your time will come. Because it will.

Associate with positive, go-getting people.

Ask for advice. Everyone has something to teach you.

9

You're Back — Handling the Process

The Interview

When we're working, preparing for an interview is just another thing on your list. To the unemployed, however, it's the biggest thing to happen since, well, the day we were made unemployed. It takes on bigger proportions because it means much more. And the longer you've been out of work, the bigger it becomes. So much so that by the time the interview day arrives, you are so keyed up that you're secretly hoping it will be cancelled! And that's no good, because you deserve success, and interviews are an important step in getting there.

Numerous books and articles have been published on how best to prepare for an interview. Here are a few additional ones for when you are coming at it as an unemployee - lessons I learned from either being the unemployed interviewee or interviewing people who were unemployed.

Tips on handling the interview

1. IF YOU HAVE AN AFTERNOON INTERVIEW, DON'T WALK IN LOOKING LIKE YOU'VE ONLY JUST SHOWERED

That has 'unemployed' written all over it. Shower and dress in the morning, just as you would do if you were working, so that when you come in you have a 'productive' look about you.

2. DON'T SPEND DAYS PREPARING FOR THE INTERVIEW

You may come across as someone who has too much time on your hands, or is desperate, and over-do the sales pitch. Two to three hours' preparation in total should be more than sufficient.

3. DON'T ATTACH SO MUCH IMPORTANCE TO THE INTERVIEW THAT IT BECOMES BIGGER THAN IT REALLY IS

Prepare, be confident, do your best to sell yourself, and then leave it in their hands. And do as many interviews as possible, including for jobs that you may not want. The experience will prove extremely useful.

4. DON'T OVER-TALK

When interviews are the only reason we have for leaving the house, we run the risk of over-compensating for this at interviews, often by over-talking. Interviewers can only take in so much from one meeting with you, and again, it can make you look desperate. Think before you speak. Speak slowly and deliberately. Don't assume that the interviewer's silence is an invitation to talk further. It rarely is. So give clear, considered answers to his or her questions and then stop. If you encounter a silence, ask: 'Have I answered that sufficiently?' Or let them come back with further questions.

5. BE POSITIVE

I've said this before and I'll say it again. Be positive about the role, about the company, and about its achievements. Don't feel as though you need to do a full audit on its strengths and weaknesses, however. Remember, it is very easy to criticise the work of others, so don't go into the interview with a list of things you would change about the company just to show them how insightful you are. They are looking for someone to fit in, after all. Mentioning one or two possible 'improvements' is quite enough.

6. USE YOUR PREPARATION TIME PRODUCTIVELY

This sounds obvious, I know, but I found that this came more easily when I was working than when I was not. I *did* spend hours thinking about the interview and worrying about it, but not enough time, pen, phone and internet to hand, actually *preparing* for it.

So for those of you who may be a little out of practice, don't go to the interview until you have clear answers to the following questions:

Who is interviewing you?

What does the company do? And for which types of customers?

What does it do well?

What challenges does it face?

What is happening in their industry?

Who is their competition?

What does the advertised role require?

How will your particular skills and achievements help you meet these requirements?

Why do you think you would be great at this job, and what hard evidence do you have to back this up?

Much of this information is available from the agency, the company website, the internet, brochures and employees of the company, if you can find them. Don't be afraid to make some phone calls and push for information. When you're not working and can't ask people in the office, you have to push harder. But do push. It doesn't take long to make a few calls. You may not get perfect answers, but it's better than nothing.

Handling the Difficult Questions

Questions on your employment status are all about you, your attitude and your maturity. Prospective employers have every right to ask, so don't bristle when the subject arises. Typical questions you could be asked are:

Why did you lose your job?

How were things with your employer when you left? (i.e. Did it end badly?)

Why have you been unemployed for so long?

What are you doing with your time?

How are you handling being unemployed?

How has the situation changed you?

How you handle tough question such as these are just as important as the answer itself, so watch your tone of voice, facial expressions and general demeanour. These things give away more than you think. The best advice here is to be positive but not overtly so. And be confident but not arrogant. A calm, measured confidence comes across when you truly believe in yourself, your achievements and your strengths.

QUESTION 1: HOW DID YOU HANDLE BEING LET GO?

The best way to answer this question is honestly, and by keeping it short and sweet. This is particularly true if your previous job ended badly. *Do not say anything negative.*

Answer: 'It was tough, of course, for all of those affected, but it was also a difficult decision for the management and I think they handled the process as well as they could. I didn't take it personally as I know that they were always very happy with my performance. The business needs just changed, and with that, the need for my role, and many other roles, disappeared.'

If you reacted badly to the decision to let you go and acted inappropriately, don't mention it. Forget it. Retain a positive tone. Remember, whatever may have happened is yesterday's news, and your prospective employers probably have better things to be doing than dredging through your past. They will be judging you on how you come across to them today: your attitude, your amount of belief in yourself, your level of preparation for the interview and your ability to sell your experience to them. Don't be weighed down by the past; nobody else is. You've learned important lessons and you've earned the right to move on.

QUESTION 2: WHY HAVE YOU BEEN OUT OF WORK FOR SO LONG?

If the market for your particular skill is tight, don't be afraid to say so. During an economic downturn, marketing, HR, training, technical support, R&D and all back-office functions are the hardest hit. If you also have the misfortune of having a 'broad-stroker' CV, you'll find the going even harder.

Answer: 'As a [name your profession], the recession reduced the number of opportunities in my area. It is equally difficult for many of my experienced colleagues in the sector who are also struggling to find a good job, like the one I have applied for. However, I have been keeping myself productive with [mention the important things you are doing with your time].

QUESTION 3: WHAT HAVE YOU BEEN DOING WITH YOUR TIME?

Answer: 'Apart from actively looking for opportunities like this one, I have also taken time out to [list all the ways in which you made your free time matter – training, volunteering, child-rearing and other family commitments, part-time work, hobbies, interests, pursuit of goals, and so on].' Speak proudly about it. Make it matter, because it does. Include in your answer how these activities contributed to your life, and explain what you learned in the process.

QUESTION 4: ARE YOU STILL IN TOUCH WITH YOUR EX-EMPLOYERS?

Answer: 'Yes, I made some great friends and see them regularly.'

QUESTION 5: WHY WERE YOU CHOSEN FOR REDUNDANCY?

Answer: 'It was simply a business need. In the light of the tough market situation, the management decided that certain goals/initiatives/activities were no longer as urgent as they had been previously. The company had been scaling back in other areas for quite some time, so we saw it coming.'

Alternative answer: 'They simply shut down the division/team where I worked. While the division/team made significant contributions to the organisation [list the key achievements], it was no longer regarded as business-critical for the company in the short term. The company had been scaling back in other areas for quite some time, so we saw it coming.'

Finally, take every opportunity to mention your contribution to the organisation and the friendships you made there.

Topics to Avoid

1. IF YOU WERE FIRED

Answer: 'I enjoyed working in such a dynamic and fast-changing environment and I believe I achieved a lot in the time I was there. Unfortunately, the role I took was not what I had expected it to be, and it changed quite a bit during my time there. However, as I said, I achieved [mention three important things] and made some good friends.'

2. IF YOU WERE A VICTIM OF MANAGEMENT INCOMPETENCE

Answer: 'I contributed to a number of important decisions and activities during my time there [mention a few]. However, the company faced serious challenges and many areas were affected, including the area I worked in.' Again, mention that you also made some good friends.

3. IF YOU TOOK LEGAL ACTION AGAINST A PREVIOUS COMPANY

This almost goes without saying: don't say a word about it, unless they already know about it and specifically ask for an explanation.

Answer (and only if pushed to the wall): 'It was a very difficult decision, as I had never been in that position before. I only had positive experiences prior to this. Out of respect for everyone involved, I will not go into too much detail. However, some serious issues arose in the company, most of which had arisen before my time, but my reputation/credibility/position came under attack [or 'many of the commitments promised by the company were not met'] for reasons I am still unsure about, and this had a negative impact on me over time. Despite numerous attempts to resolve the issue within the company, I was eventually left with no option but to seek an external resolution.'

Managing the 'Time Gaps' in Your CV

Time gaps in your CV are an obvious talking point, and prospective employers have a right to ask about them. Time gaps are created through unemployment, ad hoc contracting, travelling, ill health, further education and family commitments. Such gaps are a common feature of many working lives today. Some gaps are easy to explain, like travelling, family commitments and further training. However, there are also simple ways to manage time gaps which appear due to unemployment, so that they don't become a major talking point in the interview.

1. FILL IN AS MANY OF THE GAPS AS POSSIBLE

There are lots of ways you can do this. They include:

unpaid work relevant to your job application – assisting small businesses and doing volunteer work

hobbies/interests which are providing some income – design, website design, gardening, teaching, product testing

training/further education will also look good

2. Be Less Specific About Start and End Dates on Your CV

If you have a three-month gap here and a two-month gap there, close it off by giving the year or season you worked on the job, rather than the specific dates. Most interviewers are not going to count the days you worked in a company; they are more interested in your contribution to that company.

3. Don't Over-explain

Have an answer ready and deliver it sincerely and positively, then stop.

4. Don't Lie

Especially if this means that you put your employment at risk by lack of disclosure. This is particularly true for roles which carry public responsibility, e.g. in educational, medical, security, policing, legal or finance settings.

The main point about interviews is not to let your unemployment, or the reasons for it, weigh too heavily on your mind. Remember, you are a wiser, more mature person than you were when you were last working. Remember your achievements, the confidence you had when you worked on your most successful projects, and the wisdom you have acquired from your recent experience. Taken together, this counts for a lot.

But Is the Company Right for You?

When we are desperate to get back to work, as I was, we tend not to scrutinise the company for which we hope to work as much as we might have done when we were working. This is a mistake. The more you ask, the more you will understand about the company. Any answers they give you, however, should not turn you off the role. Quite the opposite, in fact. You just want a heads-up so that you can mentally prepare for the challenges ahead. No company is perfect. No manager is perfect. You're not perfect. And that's OK. So ask some or all of these questions:

1. WHAT ARE THE OBJECTIVES OF MY ROLE?

What is expected of me in this role? How does it fit into the team? Is it a new role? If not, where did the last person go? (You are looking for their ease, openness, culture and clarity of purpose in relation to the role they are filling.)

2. WHAT SUPPORT WILL BE PROVIDED IN THE FIRST THREE MONTHS?

From your manager? From the team? (You are looking to find out more about their approach towards new staff.)

3. WHAT ARE THE MAIN PRIORITIES FOR THE COMPANY OVER THE NEXT SIX TO TWELVE MONTHS?

Short-term sales? This may indicate sales target problems.

Diversification? This may indicate a possible role change.

Growth? This may indicate long hours and changing work processes/management procedures.

Consolidation? This may indicate financial difficulties or poor performance.

4. WHAT TYPE OF CONTRACT IS IT?

It is always worth researching the types of contracts on offer, and there are many sources of information to help you. Here are some of them:

citizensinformation.ie/categories/employment/employment-rights-and-conditions/contracts-of-employment

Go Contracting in Ireland, by Eugene Houston, published by Working & Living Publications

SUMMARY OF CONTRACTS

A. AGENCY-LED CONTRACTS

Your employment contract is with the recruitment agency, not the company. You will get your salary and expenses directly from the agency. The company where you work is simply a client of the agency.

B. FIXED-TERM CONTRACT

Such a contract runs for a specified time period, beyond which the company has no legal obligation to retain the employee or pay a severance package.

C. CONTRACT OF INDEFINITE DURATION

This is essentially permanency and tends to come after either a fixed-term contract or an agreed probationary period.

D. INDEPENDENT CONTRACTOR AGREEMENT

This is where your own company employs you and is responsible for deductibles, such as tax and social insurance. The company where you work is a client of your company and pays your company an agreed gross amount.

Starting Again: A New Job – A New You

*A SUCCESSFUL PERSON IS ONE WHO CAN LAY A FIRM
FOUNDATION WITH THE BRICKS THAT OTHERS THROW AT HIM*
PSALM LXXV, V. 6

Well, it's finally happened. You've done the necessary and got yourself back into the wonderful world of work. So it's goodbye to *Dallas* re-runs, long lunches, and calling people who'd long since forgotten you, and hello to pay cheques, gridlock, long hours and new faces. It might not be the best job in the world – but then again, it might be. It doesn't matter: you're back in and on the right track.

Take off your 'I've been unemployed for-ev-errr' hat

Those who experience a bruising redundancy situation or have been unemployed, particularly for an extended period, tend to think, and often behave, differently from those who breeze from one opportunity to the next. First of all, our bruised egos give us the impression that the working world isn't as safe as we had thought, so our guard is up. We tend to work harder and take ourselves more seriously than, say, our breezier colleagues. This can be a good thing, so long as you don't try too hard or get too serious.

Below are tips on getting through the first few months of a new job, from both my own experiences and the experiences of my fellow unemployees. What's interesting about these tips is how similar they are to the lessons we had all eagerly learned (and quickly forgotten!) at the postgraduate 'Getting Your First Job' workshop we attended in college.

1. DON'T RUSH

You may feel the pressure to jump in and fix every problem, just to show everyone – and perhaps yourself too – how great you are. This is a mistake. Don't start out as the donkey, or you will always be the donkey. So take it easy. Let people continue doing their jobs. Don't interfere. Keep close to your immediate managers and take on their agenda as your priority.

2. AVOID EXTREME OPINIONS

Starting a new job is exciting but can also be nerve-racking. When we doubt ourselves, we have a greater tendency to form extreme opinions – to observe only the negative, or only the positive. When it's only negative, it's damaging to you and everyone around you. You may believe that you see practice that is below par, or notice things that appear to be missing, or people who seem not to be performing. My advice is to not make a big a deal about it initially, because you may well be wrong.

Think positively, particularly about the people you work with and, more importantly, who work *for you*. Think of them as capable, decent people who deserve your respect, until you have clear evidence to the contrary.

Ask to meet people who may be affected by your role.

Ask questions about their needs and expectations of you.

Jot your observations down on paper.

If relevant, and at an appropriate time, present the issues and, importantly, your recommendations to your immediate managers.

Get their advice and permission to implement recommendations.

Be supportive of all initiatives that are currently in train.

Extreme positivity, on the other hand, can blind you to areas where there is room for improvement, give the impression that you don't have anything new to offer or indicate that you are desperate to be liked. A respectful, supportive attitude is the best approach to take.

3. TRY TO GET A QUICK WIN WITHIN THE FIRST THREE MONTHS

First impressions are lasting, so do something with which you can be credited and which will help you build credibility and acceptance as soon as possible – ideally within your first three months, but definitely within the first six.

4. DO TRY TO BE OF ASSISTANCE TO YOUR COLLEAGUES IF THEY ARE UNDER PRESSURE

Offer your time if they require a dig-out – although obviously without taking on *so much* of their work that your own objectives are undermined. But be there for them, even if it's just to give them advice or make them a cup of coffee.

5. LEARN HOW TO TAKE INSTRUCTION

With good grace and respect. Don't resent your boss or others for laying down instructions. It's their job. Be grateful for it: it means that you will be able to achieve things quickly. However, if they want *you* to tell them how you should approach your job or project, formally present it to them for approval within an agreed time period.

6. Don't Hide Your Progress

When you are used to doing your own thing and not answering to anyone, it is easy to forget to let people know that you are making progress. Write up a weekly report on your key projects, outputs and results, however small, and circulate it to a small selection of managers.

7. Don't Avoid People

Social and interpersonal skills are as important when it comes to keeping your job as how capable you are at the job itself. So approach people positively, make small talk, socialise with them and remember their names. Give the impression that you like the people in the company, including your team. Tell people you are happy to be there and are looking forward to getting stuck in! If people ask what you did before you came in, focus only on your achievements.

8. Don't Overreact

That is: to problems, to criticism, to indifference or hostility, to your workload. If you hear negative things or experience negativity, raise it with your manager. He or she may have some insight and advice as to how you can overcome it. If not, quietly approach the person in question to see if they can come to a mutual agreement to resolve whatever the issue is. This may include helping them out in some personal way. If not, withdraw temporarily and get on with your job. Don't tolerate bad behaviour, but don't make a big issue of it either. You can only do so much.

9. Don't Try Too Hard

Don't try to make people like you. You can't solve every problem that you encounter. Acceptance of you, even in the most difficult environment, will come with time, reflecting your positive attitude and, most importantly, your achievements.

10. DON'T RE-INVENT THE WHEEL

There are work processes, tools and templates already in existence. Re-use whatever you can find.

11. APPLY YOURSELF AS PRODUCTIVELY AS YOU CAN

Be seen to be a hard worker.

12. COMMUNICATE WITH YOUR MANAGER

If you are feeling overwhelmed or confused, ask for support, direction and clarity. You have a right to do this. That's what managers are there for.

Conclusion

It's been five years since my last walk in the valley of the disappearing ego. I don't know what's around the corner, but I do know that unemployment is not the end of the world. (That said, I am hoping that I have reached my life's quotient on such experiences.) If you're still in the valley, I hope you found something useful here to help you on your journey back. And if you've been looking for a job for a long time, stay positive. You'll get there. Remember, there's always time for a comeback.

Useful Support Sites

entemp.ie/employment/redundancy/employmentrights.ie
cpl.ie
manpower.ie
hrm.ie
irishjobs.ie
loadzajobs.ie
fas.ie
nightcourses.com
postgrad.ie
enterpriseboards.ie
startingabusinessinireland.com
itsyourmoney.ie
pensionsboard.ie
Revenue.ie
creditunion.ie
welfare.ie
jumbletown.ie/forums/index.php
greenmetropolis.co.uk
ebay.ie
free-stuff.co.uk
irishopinions.com
BlogCashGuide.com
Bloggers-Guide.com
facebook.com

Acknowledgements

There are a number of people to whom I owe a debt of gratitude:

First and foremost, my many 'redundee' comrades and friends, who not only provided me with an invaluable support system during my 'time out', but also, more importantly, through their feedback and suggestions, made this book possible. Too many to mention. You all know who you are.

I would also like to thank the great team in Liberties Press, Sean, Peter, Orlaith and Caroline, who understood that handling a tough topic such as job-loss should not be heavy or depressing for the reader, but should lighten their load and perhaps make them smile.

Thanks to my husband Cormac for his constant support and encouragement. To my mum and dad, sisters, brothers and mother-in-law: thanks for all the support and dinners! To all my nephews and nieces: thanks for never caring whether I was working or not.

To my darling son Ryan, who will (hopefully) not remember the 'downturn to beat all downturns': may you always find something to laugh about, as you do right now.

Finally, thank you to my friend Leo Kearns, who propelled me back into full-time employment.

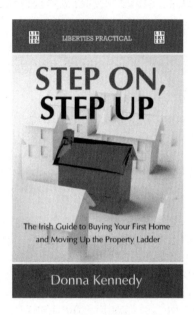

STEP ON, STEP UP
The Irish Guide to Buying Your First Home
and Moving Up the Property Ladder
DONNA KENNEDY

As the recession bites, now is an ideal time for first-time buyers
to step on to the property ladder. In this accessible guide,
property investor Donna Kennedy tells you how to negotiate the
maze of house buying and make money from property.

ISBN: 1-978-905483-61-7 | €9.99
Available from all good bookshops
Trade orders to CMD: 01 294 2560

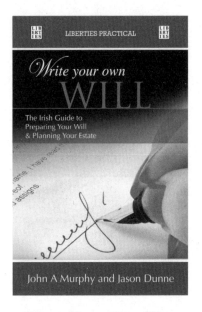

WRITE YOUR OWN WILL
The Irish Guide to Preparing Your Will
and Planning Your Estate
JOHN G. MURPHY AND JASON DUNNE

In the current economic climate, making sure your personal
affairs are in order is more important than ever. In *Write Your
Own Will*, solicitors John G. Murphy and Jason Dunne give you
the tools to write your own will. Includes sample wills.

ISBN: 1-978-905483-59-4 | €9.99
Available from all good bookshops
Trade orders to CMD: 01 294 2560